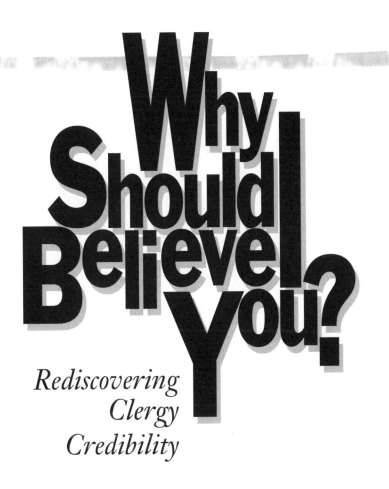

Why Should I Believe You?

Rediscovering Clergy Credibility

THOMAS G. BANDY

ABINGDON PRESS / NASHVILLE

WHY SHOULD I BELIEVE YOU?
REDISCOVERING CLERGY CREDIBILITY

This book is printed on acid-free paper.

Library of Congress Cataloging-in-Publication Data

Bandy, Thomas G., 1950-
  Why should I believe you? : rediscovering clergy credibility / Thomas G. Bandy.
    p. cm.
  ISBN 0-687-33529-9 (pbk. : alk. paper)
  1. Pastoral theology. 2. Mission of the church. 3. Church leadership. I. Title.

BV4011.3.B36 2006
262'.1—dc22

                                                                      2006027941

06 07 08 09 10 11 12 13 14 15—10 9 8 7 6 5 4 3 2 1
MANUFACTURED IN THE UNITED STATES OF AMERICA

CONTENTS

Chapter 1

A Critical View from the Outside

Chapter 2

A Faithful Response from the Inside

CHAPTER ONE

A Critical View from the Outside

The credibility of orders of ministry in established churches is at a new low. This is despite the efforts of Catholic and Protestant churches to shore up that credibility through intensive training, closer monitoring, and publicly visible acts of discipline. The church is like a child riding a bicycle. On level ground, her balance is so perfect she barely needs to touch the handlebars to steer. Now that she is rapidly accelerating down a steep hill, she is holding the handlebars tighter and tighter and screaming louder and louder. The primary reaction of the church to its own decline is more control and constant complaint. Meanwhile, the observing public is wondering why she chose to ride a bicycle in a rugged landscape in the first place.

The Crisis of Clergy Credibility in History

There is a fundamental assumption in the history of Christianity from its biblical beginnings. The assumption is usually ignored when the church is ascendant; it must be recognized and applied if a descendent church is to rise like the phoenix from its own ashes. Here it is:

> **The functions of church leadership are driven by the needs of the mission field, not by the convenience of the institutional church.**

You can observe the truth of this statement from the very ambiguity of the New Testament, as each newly planted church broke from the positions, titles, and job descriptions of both established Judaism and established paganism, reshaping and redirecting the functions of religious leadership. Even when these new churches borrowed from the Roman system of civil administration, or interpreted pagan roles for priests, seers, and prophetesses, the roles were barely recognizable once they were filled.

"Apostle" is one such role. There is no equivalent or institutional paradigm for it. It was Jonah without the need for the whale. It was Alexander without the need for an army. The unique role of the apostle was not the result of premeditated strategic planning back in the boardroom of the earliest church in Jerusalem, but simply a convergence of expectation on the part of many cultures and new churches. They did not create an office and fill it. They recognized a need and met it. The new role of the apostle was an evolution in discipleship, just as Christian mission was an extension of Christ's incarnation.

"Pastor" and "bishop" are also examples of how the mission field shapes leadership roles. Of course scholars can trace the origins of the original titles to the teaching and governance roles of small town rabbis or provincial Roman administrators, but they quickly became unrecognizable from the old contexts and were entirely reinvented for a new worldview. The pastor became a mentor, model, martyr, intermediary to the divine, and spokesperson for the Spirit. This was never imagined previously. The bishop became a church planter, spiritual authority, intermediary with civil government, and definitive interpreter of the scriptures. This was undoubtedly not predicted by Paul or Peter. The mission field demanded it.

Fundamentally, the crisis of clergy credibility today is a result of centuries of denial or indifference to this basic assumption. People of every demographic and lifestyle segment have come to disrespect both the church and its leadership because they have consistently opted for institutional convenience and have failed to adapt to the changing needs of the mission field. For centuries, the western church has been in denial that there even was a mission field, or it assumed that the mission field was far away. The important people had already come to Christ, and all that remained was for the church to triumph among the lesser of God's people.

This profound, pervasive, unchallenged arrogance and condescension is the real root of the crisis of credibility. Its power is revealed by the fact that it has been identified again and again, acknowledged verbally by church leaders again and again, and yet nothing has broken the corporate addiction of the church to itself. The church is addicted to the church. It does not hunger and thirst for and desire unity with Jesus Christ, because it does not strive and risk and sacrifice everything to join Christ in mission. Instead, it is absorbed with itself. Our issue today is not how many angels can dance on the head of a pin. Our issue is how many clergy, with guaranteed salaries, can preserve heritage properties in the same zip code.

The church is addicted to the church. The rampant institutionalism that emerged in both the east and west after 1054, and which has unfolded for a full millennium, is a self-destructive behavior pattern, chronically denied, but constantly retrenched. And every judicial inquiry, research grant, and study guide simply feeds the church's compulsive need to focus on itself. It is a kind of narcissism that is a direct contradiction to the original mission urgency commanded by Christ. It is not a "righteous remnant," but a "self-righteous remnant." It is not a "holy huddle," but an "unholy huddle." What is holy is not the church, but the church-in-mission, because the hope of the world lies not in the ideal of Christ, but in the incarnation of Christ.

The crisis of clergy credibility today is not unique. There have been other times of crisis, which precipitated various movements of serious reform.

➤ The emergence of the monastic movement in the fourth century can be seen as a reform movement to return the church to its apostolic roots, and return church leaders to their apostolic role as mentors and spiritual guides. The credibility of church leaders had been undermined by acceptance as a state religion and the desire to exact vengeance on former persecutors. The church had become the new home of privilege and the ladder to power and influence. The monastic movement withdrew from the cultural charade to confront the *real* world of sin and death with leaders who were at once ascetic and authentic.

➤ The Gregorian reform in the late eleventh century can be seen as a reform movement to focus parish priests and regional bishops on their apostolic role to lead God's mission. The credibility of church leaders had been compromised by state investitures (appointment of church leaders by the civil authorities), the wealth of large sees, and the marriage of clergy. The church had become distracted from its true purpose to build the kingdom of God. The Gregorian reform held priests accountable to the call to shape their lifestyles around the mission, rather than to shape the mission around their lifestyles.

➤ The Protestant Reformation in the sixteenth century is the most obvious reform movement of the church, seeking to return church leaders to their apostolic roles as teachers and equippers of Christian life. The credibility of church leaders had been undermined by corrupt practices and abusive behavior. The church had become a participant in the culture of self-interest, rather than a prophetic witness to confront it. The Protestant Reformation was an articulate and sometimes violent *no!* to the excesses and pride of worldly church leaders.

➤ The Wesleyan movement in the eighteenth century is one of several regional reform movements to restore the apostolic role of indigenous ministry that challenged privilege and power. The credibility of church leaders had been undermined by irrelevant practices and ineffective traditions. The church had become a perfunctory routine and a mere tool of socialization. The Wesleyan movement pushed church leaders back into the mission for the poor, the lost, and the uncivilized world that lay beneath the veneer of civility.

It is noteworthy that the crisis of clergy credibility and the subsequent movements to reform church leadership, all occur in contexts of global and social uncertainty. At each time, revolutions in technologies are changing the historic patterns of commerce and daily living; mass migrations are creating cultural confusion; urbanization and population density are expanding the gap between rich and poor. At each time, a form of capitalism or consumerism dominates the mind-set of culture, treating humans as objects and ideas as commodities. And at each time, established church leaders consistently *fail* to confront these trends and instead accommodate themselves to culture. In other words, the decline of credibility for clergy is a kind of mirror that reflects that diminishing self-respect of the public. The reform of the one implies the reform of the other.

Every great reform movement is accompanied by "sidetracks." The reform movement does not stand alone, but at the time of its unfolding is camouflaged in the midst of other movements that are not authentic to the Christian mission. These other movements sidetrack energy and attention away from true mission purpose, but gain considerable notoriety and influence for a relatively brief time.

○ The Pelagian movement was the great sidetrack of its time and a counterpoint to the authentic monastic movement. It sought to accommodate to culture by reducing the gospel to an educational methodology and falsely restoring credibility to church leaders by making them mere philosophers and wise men.

○ The crusades launched by Urban II in 1095 (extending all the way to 1201) were the great sidetrack of their time and a counterpoint to the authentic Gregorian reform. The crusades sought to accommodate to feudal culture by reducing the gospel to spiritual warfare and falsely restoring credibility to church leaders by making them mere propagandists and fearmongers.

○ A host of utopian movements in Europe and North America in the sixteenth through eighteenth centuries were the great sidetracks of that time and counterpoints to the authentic Protestant reform. They sought to accommodate to expansionist political policies by reducing the gospel to sectarian communities and falsely restoring credibility to church leaders by making them otherworldly visionaries beyond the reach of civil justice.

○ The "John Spong" movement is among many sidetracks of our time (including the controversies of the "Jesus Seminar," the disputes over sexual orientation, and other ideological posturing). They are counterpoints to the authentic movements for "incarnational" religion and indigenous mission, and accommodate to the pervasive skepticism and scientism of culture. They restore clergy credibility only by merging clergy into the acceptable, politically correct, cultural climate of unbelief.

None of these sidetracks actually restored the credibility of the clergy. Yet for a time, they appeared to give the clergy some new focus and identity and provided some clarity to the public about what they should or should not expect from church leadership. Sidetracks obscure authentic reform movements. Great leaders discern this fact and lead the church to recover its sense of priorities. Thus, Augustine confronted Pelagius; Saint Francis modeled a peaceable alternative to crusades; generations of African American Christian leaders laid the foundations for social reform; and an emergent church breaks the old boundaries between liberal and evangelical theology to forge a new orthodoxy. Yet *at the time*, the boundaries between authentic reform and inauthentic sidetrack are often blurred. Can church leaders today discern the true path to restore clergy credibility?

The Crisis of Clergy Credibility Today

More than one observer of Christian history has realized that we are overdue for another reform movement. The context of cultural and social change has once again accelerated revolutions in technology, mass immigration, rapid urbanization, and rampant consumerism (with all the accompanying evils). Once again institutional church leadership has largely accommodated itself to, and participated in, these demonic forces. We are now about ninety years into another period of critical transition.

The transition began in 1914 with the collapse of the old European political orders and social stability, in which church leaders played a most supportive role. The collapse led to diminished respect for the church and its leaders and for the theology and philosophy they preached. The subsequent violence of the two world wars and many regional wars has heightened the three existential anxieties of the public beyond endurance:

- the anxiety of fate and death;
- the anxiety of emptiness and meaninglessness;
- the anxiety of guilt and condemnation.[1]

There was a time when the church, and church leaders, could credibly be considered to have authoritative responses to these anxieties. No more.

The first stage of skepticism emerged as the death of God movement in the early 1960s, partly influenced by the ideas of the world "coming of age" and the prospect of "religionless Christianity" borrowed (inappropriately) from Bonhoeffer. In a sense, John Spong is the descendant of this same movement. However, the death of God has been followed not by the birth of higher wisdom in men and women, but by the proliferation of many gods in an emergent pagan world. Church leaders lose credibility because they are seen by the public doing combat with straw men. They behave as if godless atheism is the enemy, when in fact the problem perplexing the public is not the absence of God, but the proliferation and competition of many gods.

The second stage of skepticism emerged as the "great conspiracy" movement in the 1970s. If God was dead, then the history of Christian teaching must be not only incorrect, but also intentionally misleading. Church leaders are not stupid; they are deceptive. Conspiracy theories proliferate, suggesting that a deliberate deception of the public has been perpetrated for over a millennium. The latest manifestation of the movement is the "da Vinci code" fiction, but it really began with the discovery of the Dead Sea Scrolls and wild speculation about the origins of the church, including the claim that it all started with the worship of sacred mushrooms, that the Templars have been hiding the secret of the Grail amid intentionally obscure ecclesiology, or that the Gnostic Gospels represent the real "orthodoxy" of the

Christian movement. In the view of the general public, the church is fundamentally a deceptive and disreputable organization.

The third stage of skepticism emerged as the "useless clergy" movement of the later 1980s and 1990s. If church leaders could not provide a convincing faith response to existential anxiety, and needed to dissociate themselves from disreputable organizations, what would they do in order to earn a salary? The therapeutic and nonprofit leadership roles seemed the only way to regain credibility. Yet an unending string of moral abuses, and a lack of competitive and cross-sector professional training, made clergy second-class therapists and unreliable nonprofit CEOs at best. In the emerging world of professionalism, they became increasingly "useless" to the public.

The order in which these three stages of skepticism have emerged is important. This transitional period has seen major paradigm shifts that ultimately lead to the credibility crisis of clergy:

- ✓ from the death of God to the belief in many gods;
- ✓ from the irrelevancy of the church to the conspiracy of the church;
- ✓ from the oddity of clergy to downright distrust or disrespect of clergy.

What seemed outdated, irrelevant, or simply odd in 1950 has become fearful, obstructive, and hostile in the new millennium. In just under sixty years, the credibility of the church has plummeted. Yet it is important to understand what came first. It's not that clergy credibility declined, and then belief in God declined, but the reverse. Therefore, the restoration of confidence in clergy will not come from defining their professional roles, or from restructuring the programs or polities of the church. It will come when the public becomes convinced that

Christian faith can overcome the three fundamental anxieties of existence.

My approach is quite different from the interpretations of ordered ministry that historically have shaped the job descriptions of clergy. Those interpretations were done *from inside the organization*, so that the definition and deployment of ordered ministry would be consistent with the systematized theology and historical practice of the church. This was appropriate in Christendom. However, with the passing of Christendom, it is more appropriate to assess the credibility of ordered ministry *from the outside*, namely, from the point of view of the emerging pagan public toward whom Christian mission is directed. They are the ones who will ultimately decide which Christian leaders are "credible" and which are not.

Who Is the "Public"?

One of the great challenges of the emerging pagan world is that it is so diverse. There are multiple "publics," for whom spirituality and culture have merged into literally thousands of different forms. In the Christendom world, we could assume that where two or three are gathered together, there is Christ in the midst of them. It did not require a very broad sampling of opinion to assess the point of view of the public. In the brief time following the two world wars when God was dead and secularity dominated culture, we could assume that where two or three were gathered together, a *universal rejection of Christ* was in the midst of them. And it still did not require a very broad sampling of opinion to assess the point of view of the public. In the emerging pagan world, however, we must assume that where two or three are gathered together, there is a unique microculture with a unique spirituality, which does not necessarily connect with other microcultures.

The point is that, simply in the context of spirituality, there is no "public." There are many, many "publics." That means that the definition of "credibility" is a moving target, and that denominational assumptions that credibility can and should be standardized will inevitably be frustrated. The situation is akin to that of the first six centuries of the earliest church in which various regions recognized various prophets, prophetesses, bishops, elders, shepherds, mystics, monks, and mendicant teachers. A comparison of what constituted "credible" leadership among Montanists and Orthodox adherents would be a relevant study today. However, our situation differs from the ancients in one crucial way. The first six centuries saw leaders self-consciously consolidating and systematizing Christian culture, and it appears that at least the first six years of the new millennium are experiencing the fragmentation and deconstruction of a uniform Christian culture.

When we look beyond the small minority of "true believers" who support the declining North American church with time and money, there are two kinds of public.

➤ The shrinking minority are people with Christian memory. The spectrum of this group ranges from people who are regular worshipers and who know and appreciate the basics of Bible, doctrine, and history; to people who have had some involvement with the church at least in childhood and still value the authority of the church to influence their life and lifestyle decisions. In the interest of brevity, I shall refer to this public as PCMs ("people with Christian memory").

➤ The growing majority are people with no Christian memory. The spectrum of this group ranges from people who have lapsed from Christian connection, forgotten or rejected whatever they once knew, for whom the authority of the church has virtually no decisive influence; to people who are spiritually alive and seeking, but Christianity as a religion is of little interest compared to the many other spiritual options available. These are the "spiritually yearning, institutionally alienated" people about whom I have written so much. I shall refer to this public as SYiAs, who say to the church "See ya later—probably when pigs fly and hell freezes over!"

PCM: People with Christian Memory
SYiA: Spiritually Yearning, Institutionally Alienated

Within these two kinds of public there are innumerable other "publics." Their affinities, issues, and needs are always changing and reforming. With varying degrees of commitment they explore many religions and spiritualities. However, they are all driven by the three existential anxieties and their inability to cope with them and overcome them. They all share the growing doubt that church leaders will be much help.

What Does "Credibility" Mean?

The biggest mistake post-Christendom church leaders make is that they assume both of these publics are stupid. They make this mistake over and over and over again in every condescending sermon and pompous public policy statement, and it infuriates both the PCMs and the SYiAs. People with Christian Memory are furious that the church, and its institutional representatives in ordered ministry, assumes that they cannot be "called by God" into profound mission that is equally important to that of any ordered minister. Spiritually Yearning Institutionally Alienated people are furious that the church, and its institutional representatives, assumes that churches deserve more attention by virtue of their status in the eyes of the government, which has granted them exclusive nontaxable benefits.

Both publics are more intelligent, better educated, more sophisticated, more sensitive to cultural nuance and ethical dilemma, and more spiritually alive than the established church routinely assumes. In this, the church today is very different from the church of the first six centuries of the Christian era. The ancient church was profoundly respectful of the public. The church addressed the public as colleagues in a spiritual quest and even trained its missionaries to understand religious differences and model (that is, risk their lives for) an alternative lifestyle centered on Christ.

These two publics may not articulate their critique of the church in formal protests and letters of complaint. They simply disappear. Yet as they go, if you listen to their conversations, you discover they all measure credibility in four basic categories:

> **Attitude:** Both publics respect leaders with a clear missional purpose, who are prepared rigorously to align even the smallest detail of their lives to pursue and deliver that mission *and nothing else.* Credibility means that no sidetracks are tolerated. The leader cannot be deflected from his or her purpose by the temptations of affluence or ego. They are "straight arrows" flying to the target.

The reason fewer people go to seminary or dedicate their lives to parish ministry is that both publics see the clergy consistently sidetracked to protect membership privileges instead of pursuing God's mission. They simply do not reveal an attitude that commands respect.

➤ **Integrity:** Both publics respect leaders who clearly articulate and model the "DNA" of their organization. They respect leaders who hold themselves and other colleagues accountable to the boundaries of core values and shared faith convictions. If the boundaries change, they evolve through *conversation* rather than through *confrontation*. Leaders consistently and predictably operate in certain ways. As the arrow flies, they are "feathered to perfection."

The reason nobody listens to church pronouncements on public policy is that both publics experience clergy behavior as, at best, eccentric and, at worst, abusive or destructive. "Clergy bashing" is now the preferred sport of other clergy. The pagan public no longer requires lions in the arena to do the job. Clergy simply do not practice habitual, mutual accountability that commands respect.

➤ **Skills:** Both publics respect leaders who are good at what they do and get positive results. The key is not so much the skills they have, but their readiness to acquire new skills. It is not education that they respect, but *continuing education*. The public accepts the fundamental incompetence of church leaders because that is normal in every sector today. What they respect is the passion and dedication to *keep pace with the competencies of other sectors*.

The reason church decline undermines credibility for clergy is that both publics logically blame a leader for organizational failure. In a world of intense spiritual yearning, how can the public interpret the death of a church except by blaming a leader who refuses to learn how to do his or her job better? Clergy simply do not demonstrate a readiness to keep "up to speed" with all other sectors that commands respect.

➤ **Teamwork:** Both publics respect leaders who can work with one another and with the world. They respect leaders who can set aside ego and agenda to collaborate in the accomplishment of a common goal. In the case of spiritual leaders in particular, they respect leaders who can elevate the "Spirit" above the "program" or "ministry," flexibly customizing tactics in obedience to a "higher power."

The reason professionals in other public sectors (for example, health care, social service, business, and government) are so hesitant to work with the church is that they fear the antics of the church. They fear the internal power struggles, idiosyncratic behavior, obsession with trivialities, and general self-centeredness of church leaders will embarrass them or compromise their own well-defined values and convictions. Clergy simply do not function in team-building ways that command respect.

If the gospel and its messengers can be compared to a priceless jewel in an intricate and secure setting, then the credibility of the messengers becomes crucial to the acceptance and celebration of the gospel. The media is not the message. The messenger is the message. And the messengers do not command much respect.

The Irish missionaries (personified in St. Patrick, who converted the Norse and Germanic tribes) and the Byzantine missionaries (personified in the brothers Cyril and Methodius, who converted the Slavs and Magyars) and even the nineteenth-century Methodists who converted the American frontier would all understand this crucial importance of credibility. The gospel could sparkle for itself, but only if it was delivered in a setting that was stable, authentic, and durable enough to be worn around the neck or on a ring finger. Cynical historians are probably right that acceptance of Christianity by pagan nations was probably the result of political negotiation rather than the authentic conversion of kings, but that was never true of common, ordinary people. The *people* required nothing less than credibility from the missionaries.

Beyond these four essential criteria, there is considerable diversity between and among the two publics. The leader who is credible to one microculture may not be credible to another. In such a world, the Byzantine model makes a good deal more sense than the Roman model makes.

- The eastern or Byzantine model demanded that the patriarch make sure candidates were credible in the four categories above, but allowed the local village or congregation to then select its own priest or deacon. Despite our modern perceptions of the theological "councils" and slow decision-making processes, their system simply ensured consistency around attitude, integrity, skills, and teamwork and left everything else to the discretion of the local people.

- The western or Roman model (which we generally follow in North America to this day) insisted that the pope or bishop always knew best what the local people needed and could appoint specific candidates to specific locations. Despite our modern exaggerations about the efficiency of a command structure, the basic system of appointment mainly focused on controlling the everyday behavior of ordinary people. It was more concerned that a tithe was sent to the central office and that loyalty was rewarded with extra privileges. At worst, the Roman model saw bishops preoccupied with everything else in organizational life *except* attitude, integrity, skills, and teamwork.

We begin to see the reason that episcopal appointment processes broke down in ancient times and inevitably break down today. The need to control and the compulsion to micromanage is simply not suitable for a world of constant change that relies on leadership credibility.

How Does the Public Assess Credibility?

The revolution of the emerging postmodern world is even more powerful than past reformations because the Roman model is actually being dismantled and not simply corrected. The institutional church (denominations and their local franchises) still does not fully understand the extent of the revolution. It labors over detailed job descriptions that list tasks to do, responsibilities to perform, and privileges to enjoy, and fails to understand that both PCMs and SYiAs don't really care. What is important to them is *credibility*. As long as a leader has the attitude, integrity, skills, and ability to work in a team, these publics simply do not need a well-defined job description. They have a reason to trust, and that is all they require.

The problem is that neither the PCMs nor the SYiAs are very clear about *how* they assess credibility. How do you know someone has it? How do you convince somebody else that this leader has it, while that other leader does not? The following chart identifies and contrasts the key questions that are asked to determine credibility.

SYiA	PCM	Institutional Church
Questions about Religion		
How do I experience miracles?	How do we see God in the world?	How is biblical experience real today?
Is there proof?	Does it make sense?	Is it consistent with theology?
What is the record of spiritual life?	What would Jesus do?	Is it already in the Old and New Testaments?
Is it ancient and celebrity endorsed?	Would my grandparents like it?	What would Wesley (or Luther, Calvin, etc.) say?
Questions about Leadership		
Is (s)he associated with miracles?	Is he or she inspired by God?	Is he authorized to interpret the Bible?
Is (s)he convincing?	Is he or she intelligible?	Is he a skilled oral communicator?
Does (s)he live a good life?	Does he or she pray often and well?	Does he care for the flock?
Does (s)he quote real life?	Does he or she quote dead experts?	Does he quote the right people?

Methodists and church historians will note that these questions are roughly framed in the template of the Wesleyan Quadrilateral. The truth is discerned with reference (in order) to scripture, history, reason, and spiritual experience. The four reference points are not equal in church practice, however, and function more as descending layers of interpretation. The difficulty is that both publics have reversed the order of priority.

The publics do not first look to scripture. Indeed, most people don't know anything about it, and even the great biblical stories, metaphors, and ideas have dropped out of modern literature and ordinary conversation. PCMs and SYiAs will value history differently, but neither will follow *church* history very closely. Reason is important, but authentic spirituality is associated more with mystery than with clarity. In the end, experience is the most important criterion to determine credibility. Intuition, gut feeling, personal relevance, synergy, synchronicity, coincidence, and luck are crucial. When it comes to judging the credibility of spiritual leaders, this is the order of importance:

Supernatural Experience: The SYiAs will look for miraculous confirmations and portents, and PCMs will look for hidden purposes amid ordinary things. Only the institutional church seeks to justify spiritual experience today in biblical precedents of yesteryear.

Reasonable Explanation: The SYiAs expect the explanation to be in prose and "how-to" manuals, and PCMs expect it to be in poetry, music, and liturgy. Only the institutional church expects truth to be synonymous with systematic theology.

Historical Continuity: The SYiAs study ancient history in both profound and shallow ways, and the PCMs study their immediate tribal genealogy. Only the institutional church limits its study to explicitly western church history.

Record of Spiritual Life: The SYiAs search the oral and written traditions of all religions, and the PCMs limit their research to broadly Christian (usually post–sixteenth-century) sources. Only the institutional church limits its search to the Bible alone.

These contrasts explain the paradox of every seminary graduation or ordination ceremony. The church lines up candidates for certification and declares that they are "credible leaders," and they all go forth into the mission field to discover that they are not credible to the general public. The seminaries and denominations react by adding Doctor of Ministry degrees and layering more evaluation procedures on the clergy, and still they are not credible to the general public. The public asks different questions. The public evaluates credibility differently than does the institutional church.

A closer look at these contrasts provides a useful background to understand why the designations and offices of church leadership are increasingly irrelevant to the public and how the church might adjust. Note that the three columns of contrast all indicate a unique gender bias. The SYiA generation is no longer even bothering to debate supposed distinctions between male and female leadership. Credibility is a "unisex" experience. The PCMs claim to have equal expectations of male and female leaders, but, in practice, they do not. They continue to harbor hidden assumptions that place males before females. The institutional church has never made a systemic shift in thinking, despite changes in the wording of policy. They think male.

The first set of contrasts reveals that the postmodern publics have reversed the priority of the Wesleyan Quadrilateral that was broadly based on enlightened modernity. This is particularly relevant to evaluating the essential *attitude* of the leader.

SYiA	PCM	Institutional Church

The Essential Attitude about Religion

How do I experience miracles?	How do we see God in the world?	How is biblical experience real today?

The Essential Attitude about Leadership

Is (s)he associated with miracles?	Is he or she inspired by God?	Is he authorized to interpret the Bible?

The institutional church still anchors credibility on biblical knowledge and relevance. Credibility *assumes* that biblical reference is the key to interpreting daily life and that only well-trained and well-intentioned experts can interpret that Bible. The postmodern public has rejected that position, *including* the PCM segment that still maintains membership in a church. They associate credibility with some form of personal association with, or surrender to, the power of the Holy Spirit. For some, this literally means that miracles happen through or around them. People are literally healed or transformed; circumstances are instantaneously changed or redirected. For others, this means that the leader can somehow uplift the heart and instill hope for personal and social history. This is a leader who literally keeps people from committing suicide and reshapes attitudes and lifestyles.

The second set of contrasts reveals how the postmodern publics evaluate the essential *integrity* of the leader. This has particular bearing on education strategies for church leadership. The institutional church still assumes that credibility depends on theological sophistication and preaching abilities. These remain core requirements in seminary training and are fundamental to future job placement processes. Congregations and denominations demand to hear a candidate preach and quiz them about his or her theological correctness. Yet the average church member (or PCM) is no longer interested in these. These members want to know if a candidate can "make sense" of the faith and daily living, and if he or she can be intelligible in pulpit, Bible study, or daily conversation.

SYiA	PCM	Institutional Church
The Essential Attitude about Religion		
Is there proof?	Does it make sense?	Is it consistent with theology?
The Essential Attitude about Leadership		
Is (s)he convincing?	Is he or she intelligible?	Is he a skilled oral communicator?

Meanwhile, SYiAs are even more demanding than PCMs. They expect a Christian leader to demonstrate or prove his or her faith claims with verifying evidence, reliable witnesses, or the endorsement of other spiritual celebrities. Credibility means more than the ability to proclaim powerfully, or live meaningfully, but is tied to demonstrable results in the world.

The third set of contrasts reveals how postmodern publics evaluate the essential *skills* of church leadership. The center of gravity has shifted from the credibility of church leadership *in worship* to the credibility of church leadership *in life*. Life skills—or more specifically, *spiritual* life skills—are more important than worship skills.

SYiA	PCM	Institutional Church

The Essential Attitude about Religion

What is the record of spiritual life?	What would Jesus do?	Is it already in the Old and New Testaments?

The Essential Attitude about Leadership

Does (s)he live a good life?	Does he or she pray often and well?	Does he care for the flock?

The institutional church still associates credibility with the dynamic of worship as a function of pastoral care, and pastoral care as an extension of worship. Denominations expect their leaders to take church members into the distant corners of the Bible and accompany their members through the minutia of every life cycle until they die. More important, they expect that doing so will earn the respect of members and seekers and are startled when it does not. PCMs are less interested in the Bible than they are in Jesus Christ (his life, teachings, and purpose). They are more interested in the prayer life of a leader both in worship and through the week. Once again, SYiAs are even more demanding. Credibility depends on the purity and goodness of a leader revealed in the spontaneity and stress of daily living. They expect a church leader to be "better" than the average person, and they will compare that church leader to all other examples of the spiritual life in all other religions.

The fourth set of contrasts reveals how postmodern publics evaluate the essential *teamwork* of church leaders. Credibility does depend on some form of historical or social continuity, but the nature of that continuity has changed.

SYiA	PCM	Institutional Church

The Essential Attitude about Religion

SYiA	PCM	Institutional Church
Is it ancient and celebrity endorsed?	Would my grandparents like it?	What would Wesley (or Luther, Calvin, etc.) say?

The Essential Attitude about Leadership

SYiA	PCM	Institutional Church
Does (s)he quote real life?	Does he or she quote dead experts?	Does he quote the right people?

The institutional church defines the "team" very narrowly and often unpredictably. On the one hand, the institutional church refers only to the founders of its particular tribe. On the other hand, the church wants its leaders to align with whatever politically correct authority figure is in vogue in any particular region, at any particular time. Neither has any credibility for postmodern people. PCMs want the team to include their own grandparents (or their idealized perception of their grandparents) and an eclectic collection of experts in various fields who are preferably dead and cannot change their minds about anything. In other words, the most credible team is the one that best protects the status quo. SYiAs want the team to include ancient authorities (or Hollywood's version of ancient voices). They also connect the credibility of the leader with an ability to team with other active, accessible, credible people. Despite the hype about cult leaders, postmodern people are a good deal more skeptical of charismatic leaders than modern people were. Whenever they see a leader, they do not see an individual. They see a continuity of associates, which may, or may not, lend credibility to the individual.

Learning the lessons of leadership credibility helps us understand the amazing popularity of Pope John Paul II, not only among faithful Catholics, but among Protestants and seekers of all spiritualities. His legacy remains strong despite the fact that Catholic policies on many issues continue to be criticized and Catholic priests are held in no higher regard than before. Pope John Paul II embodied the principles of leadership credibility. His life and teachings connected with the key questions raised by both postmodern publics.

People with Christian Memory (PCMs) were convinced that he was inspired by God, even if some statements or policies seemed doubtful. He knew intuitively "what Jesus would do." Even when his sermons were unintelligible, his life and witness made sense. He prayed often, and Christians of every persuasion were convinced he meant every word. He was the grandparent and mentor every boomer wished he or she had.

Seekers alienated from the church (SYiAs) were convinced that miracles of personal transformation and social change followed him wherever he went. From testimonies of personal healing to the collapse of communism, people believed that John Paul II had something to do with it. His spiritual life resembled the life stories of hardship, humility, sacrifice, and generosity that are associated with saints of every religion. He was a kind of "living proof" for the power of the gospel.

Both groups found Pope John Paul II to be highly credible in all four categories. His attitude was clearly missional toward people beyond his own tribe. His integrity was beyond dispute, even to those who disagreed with his positions. His relational skills helped him connect with people of all ages and cultures. And despite his personal charisma, he gathered a team of extraordinary advisers and worked well with leaders of all religions. His credibility escalated during a time when the credibility of church leadership in general was declining, undermined by sidetracks, scandals, incompetence, and internecine feuding. He did not attract postmodern people by his biblical expertise, theological sophistication, impressive preaching, or even his pastoral attention to

members of his own flock. He attracted postmodern people by
his credibility.

The Success and Failure of Church Growth

The church growth movement has been a central feature of
Christianity in North America since western expansion in the
early nineteenth century. The current popularity of "multi-site
ministry" is the resurrection of an old denominational strategy.
The amazing thing about the church growth movement is not
that it has succeeded or failed, but that it has done both extremely
well.

- On the one hand, the church growth movement has seen
  the rise of huge megachurches and, more recently, the
  multiplication of newly planted churches and micro faith
  communities. The numbers of churches planted, new-
  comers welcomed, members added, and lives seemingly
  transformed are staggering. Judging by the statistics
  alone, one would expect North America and the world to
  have been transformed in every public sector. Therein lies
  the problem.

- On the other hand, despite the church growth movement,
  churches are closing at an escalating rate. The numbers of
  church amalgamations, member dropouts, angry or disap-
  pointed seekers, and lives that are crushed under growing
  poverty, hunger, and disease are staggering. Alternative
  church growth is fueled by disgruntled or abused traditional church people. Too often the cycle of abuse is simply repeated, and the PCMs and SYiAs spin away from the
  church altogether. Judging by these statistics alone, society
  should have seen increasing examples of mass despair.

In truth, we are seeing both things happen at once. On the one hand, mass euphoria and optimism; on the other hand, mass isolationism and fear.

What does this say about the leadership assumptions of the church growth movement? It suggests that, despite all the literature on leadership, the fundamental posture of modernity remains normative in the life of the Christian movement. The most creative, dynamic, and credible leadership is inevitably drawn into a process of western-style (Roman) institutionalization that cannot maintain the momentum of a "movement."

The best metaphor to describe the dilemma of church growth is to refer to the function of a *gravity well* in physics. A gravity well is some source of gravitational pull that diverts any moving object in space from its intended orbit or trajectory, drawing it down into a black hole of nonexistence. In the context of the Christian movement, the gravity well of church growth is the pervasive, hidden assumptions of westernized Christianity that demand the institutionalization of both church and church leadership. Seekers are attracted to Christ, but are drawn into a black hole of lost identity and purpose and accelerating obligation and sacrifice. Those who survive or bypass the gravity well replace westernized Christian memory with a more globalized Christian memory (informed more by the east and south than by the north and west). They say good-bye to the institution in all its forms, traveling on in a distinctively different, closer companionship of Christian accountability.

The key is to focus on the credibility of Christian leadership, rather than on the job descriptions or offices of Christian leadership. Only the credibility of a leader (shaped around mission attitude, integrity for values and beliefs, constant learning disciplines, and trusted teamwork) can lead Christians to escape the gravity well of westernized institutionalism. The church growth movement, like its denominational parents and partners, has never really escaped the gravity well of hidden western assumptions about what "faith community" looks like. It quickly became absorbed in the same "professionalism" about property, program, and personnel management as everyone else. Only when leaders let go of these assumptions and preoccupations can they lead the Christian movement to thrive in the pagan (non-Christendom) world.

What the chart below does not reveal is the number of people who fail ever to scramble up from the depths of the gravity well. Many PCMs and SYiAs bypass it altogether, following a different path of leadership credibility. But many are also sucked into the gravity well and, unfortunately, lost forever. They may be lost to other religions or to extreme self-interest or even to despair and death. The judgment of Jesus over the "whited sepulchers" of the Pharisees (Matthew 23) and the frustration of the earliest apostles with the synagogue and Jewish Christianity (Acts 18) prefigures the alienation experienced in the emerging Christian movement from the traditional church.

Gravity Well of Church Leadership

Seek — Leadership Credibility — See ya ...

Westernized Christian Memory

Mere Professionalism

Global Christian Memory

Institutional Church

What is the insidious "gravitational pull" of Christendom that diverts the Christian movement from its intended path and eventually undermines the credibility of Christian leaders? At the most abstract level, that insidious gravitational pull is the conviction that life can be segmented into the sacred and the secular. No matter how innovative or indigenous the church growth movement in North America has become, it almost never escapes the gravity well of Christendom shaped by Western Christianity.

	Christian Institutionalism	*Christian Movement*
	Separation of the sacred and secular	Everything is sacred
Religion:	Church **Property**	Spiritual **Companionship**
	Religious **Program**	Lifestyle **Discipline**
	Certified **Personnel**	Credible **Mentors**
	Ecclesiastical **Polity**	Missional **Purpose**
Leadership:	**Orderly** Worship	**Incarnational** Worship
	Exposited Scripture	**Analogous** Scripture
	Privileged Membership	**Servant** Discipleship
	Cultural Confrontation	**Spiritual** Confrontation

Once seekers experience the gospel and joyfully receive Christ, the gravity well of Christendom (and specifically *western* Christendom) draws their energy into the four *P*s (property, program, personnel, and polity). It seems perfectly logical and inevitable to the western mind. *Of course* we need to acquire and maintain property, especially if that property has a unique architecture and floor plan that distinguishes holy ground from profane work space. *Of course* we need to develop curricula and repetitive programs that can be budgeted, managed, and monitored to accomplish good work. *Of course* we need salaried personnel, with protected pensions and health care plans, who are trained and authorized to manage the property and the programs. *Of course* we need an ecclesiastical manual to standardize policy and practice to ensure quality control.

All these seem obvious to the Roman mind. If the newly converted seekers (now "members") have been drawn into the gravity well, so also have the Christian missionaries who converted them. Someone needs to be trained to maintain orderly, theologically correct, uniformly applied worship. Someone needs to be authorized to interpret God's Word. Someone needs to be sent to reward the dutiful members with immediate care giving, financial perks, and behavioral incentives. Someone needs to lead the charge to confront culture and make sure the sacred is never profaned by the secular.

It is all quite logical *if the pagan world is clearly being civilized into the Christian world.* But what if the opposite is happening? What if the civilized Christian world is in the process of fragmenting back into a pagan world? The PCMs and the SYiAs are resisting and rejecting the gravity well of Christendom and are looking for an alternative way to participate in the Christian movement. If in fact there is no separation of the sacred from the secular, and if all life is sacred, then property, program, personnel, and polity are no longer obvious and inevitable. All that is really necessary is an intimate pilgrim band, a discipline for daily living, credible mentors who can guide us through ambiguity, and clarity of purpose.

If there are a whole new set of "traveling necessities" for the Christian movement, a whole new kind of Christian leadership is required. This leadership is closer to the apostolic or monastic leadership of the earliest church than to the pastoral or diocesan leadership of the Christendom world. Credible leadership means something else.

> Credible leadership mediates the "real presence" of Jesus Christ in worship and life.

> Credible leadership clarifies the struggle between sin and grace through biblical storytelling.

> Credible leadership raises expectations of members to reach out to strangers to grace.

> Credible leadership wrestles with evil within the heart and in the world.

This leadership does not require a salary, pension plan, or health benefits. More than this, it is not necessarily enhanced or inhibited by seminary training and denominational certification. It is not that these things are bad. They are merely neutral. They *may* help the credibility of a leader, or they *may not.*

The truth is that the church has been in this situation before, as early as the fourth century. The moment the drive toward institutionalization gained momentum, Christians began to resist what they perceived to be a gravity well that would sidetrack them from the Christian movement. These Christians shaped the monastic movement. It emerged as a parallel church, or alternative model, for Christian companionship. Not surprisingly, it was originally motivated by and later flourished in the Byzantine world of eastern Christianity rather than the Roman world of western Christianity, but it soon caught on in the west as well.

In the Roman world (our distant ancestor in the western church of North America), the monastic community emerged from the conviction that all life was sacred. Everything was transparent to the Holy. Property, program, personnel, and polity were not necessary. One could simply withdraw into the desert, reside in ordinary utilitarian surroundings, rigorously discipline a lifestyle around the example of Jesus, sit at the feet of a mentor, learn how to resist the devil, and reemerge to convert the heathen, to found hospitals and universities, to care for orphans and widows, to lead crusades, and to challenge the injustices of the feudal society.

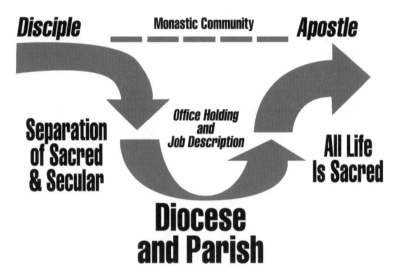

The reason the monastic movement was so threatening to the established diocesan church from as early as the fourth century through the high Middle Ages was that it questioned assumptions about apostolic succession. Who were the real successors to Peter and the original twelve apostles? The more the professional, certified clergy became preoccupied with issues of property, program, polity, and personnel, the more the Christian movement seemed to slow down. The more the amateur, authentic laity banded together in mobile communities, the more the movement seemed to accelerate outward toward strangers to grace. Monastic leaders more perfectly embodied the mediation of Christ's "real presence" in life, guidance in the struggle between sin and grace, compassion for strangers, and confrontation with the powers of evil than the diocesan leaders.

In my previous writing and teaching, the metaphorical contrast between the "Body of Christ *in residence*" and the "Body of Christ *in motion*" has been especially illuminating for People with Christian Memory (PCMs) who are increasingly skeptical of the institutional church. It is the contrast between a church of "innkeepers" and a church of "travelers" that captures their imagination. They see the gravity well that sidetracks energy, resources, and leaders ever more clearly. Behind and beneath all their criticisms of the institutional church, the key liberating insight is the conviction that "all life is sacred."

- All people are gifted by God.

- All Christians are called by God.

- All sectors of culture are caught up in the mission of God.

- All cultural forms can be used as vehicles of grace.

The separation of sacred and secular is the gravity well in its most abstract and insidious form. There are no uniquely sacred leaders; no uniquely sacred properties; no uniquely sacred programs or liturgies; no uniquely sacred music; no uniquely sacred budgets; and no uniquely sacred organizational models. Most of the things that preoccupy traditional clergy are at best sidetracks and at worst temptations of the devil. As they drop out or flee from the institutionalization of the church, they seek a different kind of faith community and a different kind of leader.

A United Methodist district superintendent once said to me ruefully that 95 percent of his time and energy, and that of the clergy within his district, was spent with the three *A*s: apportionment, appointment, and appeasement.

○ *Apportionment* is the preoccupation with unified budgets and stewardship commitments that designates a high percentage of congregational giving to judicatory finances in order to maintain salaries, pensions, and health benefits for clergy; subsidize mission by noncongregational agencies; and fund joint programs.

○ *Appointment* is the preoccupation with career path as judicatory cabinets balance privileges of seniority and mission needs and guarantee jobs in the midst of declining church membership and finances; and the constant competitiveness of clergy as they protect their incomes and aspire to more prestigious pulpits and culturally advantageous communities.

○ *Appeasement* is the preoccupation with harmony as both clergy and judicatory leaders struggle to make all the church members happy, reduce or eliminate conflict, and forge compromises about worship, mission, and leadership.

All three of these major preoccupations are related. Appeasement is necessary to maintain funding expectations for apportionments, which support the guaranteed incomes for appointments. It is crucial to appoint clergy rather than laity to leadership, since there is more control over the clergy to promote apportionments and higher motivation for clergy to be well-liked by a harmonious congregation. Ever-increasing apportionments are crucial to maintain the administrative structure of the judicatory, so that clergy who can protect the unity and financial stability of the congregations can be multiplied.

The terminology may be United Methodist, but the basic problem is universal in all established churches. Translate "apportionment" to read "unified budget" that protects the salary package and maintains church property; translate "appointment" to read "salaried staff," who are dedicated to managing the church and taking care of member needs; translate "appeasement" to read "church family," who simply must live together in perfect accord and shared aesthetic taste. My point is that this obsession with the three *A*s is precisely the gravity well that both PCMs and SYiAs observe and seek to avoid. It is noteworthy that the district superintendent with whom I discussed this was seriously considering leaving the church entirely to pursue God's mission in other ways.

I am sure that readers from within the established churches will have become angry or hostile at more than one point in this summary. After all, the growth of denominations and the training processes for clergy have developed with good and faithful intentions, and both have accomplished great things for God's mission. Many good things have been accomplished through the pooling of financial resources in a larger institutional budget. Many people have been changed, comforted, equipped, and released into mission because of the good service of traditionally trained clergy. Many congregations have discovered new depths of love and mutual support because they have sought compromises and built a deeper unity. The fact remains, however, that established churches of all kinds are declining and that contemporary North America is no longer Christendom. The ranks of skeptical PCMs and SYiAs are multiplying. It would be well to pay attention to their view from the outside.

There is a crisis in church leadership. We all know this. Seminaries are scrambling to reinvent degree programs. Foundations are investing millions of dollars to seek and develop alternatives for "education for church leadership." Denominations are redefining the orders of ministry. I have tried to suggest that the deeper dilemma is the public perception of the gravity well of church life, and that there is historical precedent in the contrast between diocesan and monastic models that helps define the issues at stake in leadership. I have identified the conditions for credibility that lie at the heart of public perceptions of church leadership.

Spiritual Leadership

Viewed from the outside, there are only two orders of ministry: disciplined membership and spiritual leadership. Public yearning and the monastic model converge. The public yearns for spiritual mentors who can help them wrestle with the devil and unite with Christ. Monastic leaders help them do precisely that without the excess baggage of property, program, personnel, and polity.

The diocesan or parish model assumes that church membership is *primarily* a privilege to receive benefits. At best it is an obligation to tithe one's life to God. A percentage of life—and always a relatively *small* percentage—is dedicated to God, and the rest can be spent as one pleases within certain prescribed boundaries dictated by institutional authorities. The most recent fad among established churches to claim that all members are ministers is recognized by SYiAs and PCMs as hypocrisy. They know that the obligation for ministry in the diocesan model really means serving on committees to define mission policy or raise mission money, but it does not really extend to actually *doing* mission or *living* a spiritual life. That is done by the handful of professionals who have been "called out" from the membership. The practical implication of this diminished obligation of membership is that the professional "orders of ministry" multiply and diversify. Leaders are ordained or commissioned to all kinds of different tasks and contexts, each one increasingly jealous of their privileges and narrowly focused on their programs. Meanwhile, privileged members are free to pursue self-interest.

The monastic model assumes that disciplined membership is one of the two basic "orders of ministry." Members are truly "brothers" and "sisters" in a rigorous, accountable, spiritual discipline that requires 100 percent of one's life. Part of that discipline is the obligation actually to participate in doing mission and to transform otherwise normal work and labor into an exercise of prayer and outreach. It is as if the church members were obligated to wear the cassock alb of a "lay brother" or "sister" as a daily "habit" even when they are working the take-out window on the late-night shift at the fast-food restaurant. The member is "called out" from culture to live and model the spiritual life in the way that clergy of the diocesan model were "called out" from the church. The lay brothers and sisters of the monastic church submit to the credible spiritual mentoring of the abbot or spiritual leader.

A monastic expectation of membership would greatly reduce the statistical calculations of adherence in the church, but greatly increase the credibility and influence of the church in the world. It would also break the church from its obsession with the three *A*s (apportionment, appointment, and appeasement). Fewer people would give to the church (since nonmembers are guests of the lay brotherhood and sisterhood), but those few people would be giving everything they had. Unity would be forged around the daily accountability of spiritual disciplines, rather than around shared aesthetic tastes or ideological points of view. Leadership would stand more firmly on credibility than office, emerging from the respect of the brotherhood or sisterhood rather than the status of an individual in the diocese.

The second order of ministry in the convergence of the seeking public and monastic model is simply spiritual leadership.

The spiritual leader is probably older, wiser, more ascetic,
more courageous, more visionary, and more compassionate than
the lay brothers and sisters themselves. He or she has more scars
from doing battle with the devil. He or she has a more beatific
demeanor from seeing more visions of Christ. He or she has a
more direct, piercing, and perhaps merciless manner from constant rigorous alignment to the will of God. His or her laughter
is more robust, tears more sorrowful, silence more profound,
words more enlightening, work more purposeful, prayers more
compassionate. These are the traits that made Antony, the great
monastic innovator, so appealing to the PCMs and SYiAs of the
fourth century.

Spiritual leaders are highly credible and therefore greatly
trusted. Because they are greatly trusted, they are free to do
whatever they think best to accomplish their mission. They are
not constrained by institutionally specified tasks or bureaucratic
demands, and indeed, if they *allow* themselves to be limited by
institutional tasks and bureaucratic demands, they lose credibility
and cease to be spiritual leaders.

This is the great dilemma for churches. Can spiritual leadership be standardized? Can it be replicated on a large scale? Can
it be nurtured, trained, deployed, and monitored, and can it
receive retirement benefits? The general public is skeptical.
They are even more skeptical when the established church multiplies orders of ministry around various tasks. Today most
denominations field a complex array of leaders: ordained and
commissioned, paid and unpaid, seminary trained and alternatively trained, full time and part time, and so on. Amid this confusing array of "offices," leaders jealously guard privileges and
titles, and hierarchies competitively protect their oversight.
PCMs and SYiAs see the gravity well of church life opening like

an abyss in front of them, and they long for the simplicity of the open road, the pilgrim band, and a credible mentor to guide them.

For example, parish clergy have generally been ordained to tasks of "word, sacrament, pastoral care, and service," with the unwritten assumption that this will be carried out on location, through ecclesiastical properties and polities, using approved programs and personnel. The public wonders what that means. What does it mean to preach in an omni-literate world? What is the significance of sacrament if all of life is sacred? Why should the church compete with therapeutic and social service nonprofits that are more expert in care giving and advocacy anyway? Why is it a priority to *pay somebody* (and support him or her with nontaxable benefits) to do things we aren't sure we need or to do things poorly that other experts can do better? The word "minister" has been stretched to fit so many people, and so many circumstances, as to be rendered nearly meaningless.

Viewed from the outside, this untenable institutional position is made even more absurd. Why should we appoint bishops and elect layers of bureaucracy to manage this seemingly pointless and confusing situation? Are they doing anything more than managing assets, defending legally recognized privileges, and keeping the clergy out of court? Is there really something else at stake here? Is there an underlying mission that is so extraordinary that no other public or corporate agency can accomplish it? The SYiA generation (unfortunately the largest and fastest-growing culture in North America) will be difficult to persuade. The PCMs are more open, provided the strategy of leadership goes back to the basics of spiritual leadership.

Viewed from the outside, the monastic model is more clearly the successor to the apostles of the earliest Christian movement. There is continuity between Jesus retreating across the sea to mentor the twelve disciples and the later emergence of the twelve apostles to travel and transform the world. It makes sense to the seeking publics that after his conversion Saul would first receive the mentoring of Ananias in Damascus, retreat into the desert for an extended period of time to wrestle with the devil and talk to the risen Christ, and only then reappear in Jerusalem and launch his mission journeys to plant new churches. Retreat and advance; go inward and then move outward; go deep and reach far; submit and then lead; discipline yourself and then discipline others; be mentored and then mentor; die to Christ and then risk martyrdom in the world. What does not make sense to the seeking public is that a true Christian disciple would unite with Christ and then buy property, settle down in relative job security, attend countless meetings, and administer a unified budget. Monks birth apostles; apostles multiply monks; they birth more apostles; and so on. That's what a "movement" does. That's why the church was originally called "The Way."

Apostolic Attitude

Attitude is everything, or is at least the foundation for all other activity. It is not a psychological state, but an existential posture toward life itself and daily living. It defines "the point of it all." It aligns the leader with the mission. Institutional churches have spent enormous energy defining the various tasks of ministry, assuming that the point of mission was clear. Yet it is no longer clear. It has not been clear in western Christianity for a millennium. Occasionally movements of reformation and renewal made it clear, but in less than a century, the gravity well of western cultural experience had replaced clarity with institutionalism again.

In the old Christendom world, the basic attitude of leadership was "pastoral." In the emerging pagan world, the basic attitude of leadership must be "apostolic." The apostolic attitude is not exclusive to the bishop. It must be the mind-set of the pastor and volunteer boards and trustees of a local congregation, the CEOs and boards of agencies supported by a denomination, and the infrastructure and membership of both. The apostolic attitude dominated the consciousness, sacrifice, and passion of spiritual leaders throughout most of the first millennium and motivated the great councils about the person and significance of Jesus the Christ. Salvation itself was at stake.

The pastoral attitude aligned leaders to a mission of waiting. It emerged in the second millennium when salvation was no longer really at stake. Preservation was at stake. Authority was at stake. Wealth was at stake. The world had been essentially "Christianized," and what remained was to wait for the Lord "between times." Comfort them through the life cycles and in the hour of their death; baptize their children and teach them what everyone knew to be true; discipline the backsliders to show greater respect and pay their dues; standardize faith and practice so that wherever mobile people traveled and worshiped they would feel right at home.

The pastoral attitude reshaped the prophetic role associated with biblical times. Prophecy became an extension of the pastoral attitude beyond the local faith community, overlaying the values and convictions of the church on the rest of society. In church there was "no longer Jew or Greek . . . slave or free . . . male and female" (Galatians 3:28), so in society as a whole there ought to be the same equality. The fact that this equality presumed unity with Christ was at first assumed, then forgotten. The attitude, however, endured. Pastors not only visited their church members in the hospital, but visited everyone else as well. They became civil servants. The mission of preservation, consolidation, and extension blurred the boundaries between evangelism and philanthropy.

The apostolic attitude aligns leaders to a mission that multiplies disciples of Jesus the Christ. It does more than draw people into a *relationship* with Christ. It draws them into *participation* with Christ in a focused mission of mystical and cultural reconciliation. It is summarized by Paul in 1 Corinthians 9:22: "I have become all things to all people, that I might by all means save some." The apostolic attitude carries an urgency that is missing in the pastoral attitude.

The apostolic attitude can best be summarized as a *fundamental preference for the stranger*, over and against a *fundamental preference for the member*. From the point of view of the apostle, "the stranger" is estranged from grace. From the point of view of the public, "the stranger" is estranged from any number of blessings. He or she is estranged from health, from peace, from justice, and from love; and yes, in the emerging pagan world, he or she consciously feels estranged from God who is the source of it all. Spiritual leaders love these "strangers" *more* than the members of the institutional church. They express the attitude of the parable in which the shepherd leaves the ninety-nine sheep that have stayed close to home in order to invest energy and risk their own lives to rescue the one sheep that has strayed.

What would an apostolic attitude look like? The following list reveals why it is so attractive to PCMs and even SYiAs who avoid the gravity well of western institutionalization.

❖ Mission first, members second (Matthew 12:48-49 and 19:27-30; Philippians 3)

> The apostolic attitude is a spontaneous, daring, habitual preference for strangers to grace. Leaders see the pagan world for what it is and refuse to be sidetracked into mere care giving for church members. *If you are a member, you*

42

are a disciple. If you are a disciple, you should be in mission to the stranger. If you are in mission, you don't need a paid professional to hold your hand all the time. This is not to say that a leader with an apostolic attitude will not retrieve, comfort, and heal a fellow pilgrim who has fallen. It is to say that the only reason the leader retrieves, comforts, and heals is that fellow pilgrims can get up and walk again on the road to mission. The apostolic attitude always has eyes for the stranger to grace.

❖ Reward innovation, not preservation (Matthew 25:14-29; Philippians 1)

The apostolic attitude reinforces mission-driven behavior, rather than maintenance-driven behavior. It rewards innovation. It may raise a salary, invest more money, advance a career, honor publicly, celebrate and learn from mistakes, and do anything practical for positive behavior modification. This is not to say that a leader with an apostolic attitude values change for change's sake. It is to say that the leader values adaptation that gets results.

❖ Lifestyle discipline, not program professionalism (Matthew 5; Philippians 2)

The apostolic attitude holds people accountable to a disciplined lifestyle that infuses work and play, personal and professional time with spiritual depth and missional purpose. Spiritual leaders shape people, not just programs. They mentor emerging missionaries. This is not to say that they do not use curricula or develop programs to teach and act, but to say that their leadership is not constrained by these programs. Their goal is to tame Eros and overcome selfishness in order to mold Christian character and inculcate selfless surrender to Christ.

❖ Spiritual growth, not smooth management (Matthew 8:19-34; Philippians 4)

The apostolic attitude encourages a corporate culture of spiritual growth and therefore of numerical and organizational growth. The goal is not to create a well-oiled institutional machine or a conflict-free and harmonious environment, but to generate a creatively stressful atmosphere of experimentation, imagination, and prayerful adventure. This is not to say that the leaders should not be good organizers, but to say that leaders should be better mentors.

❖ Team accountability, not hierarchical uniformity (John 13:1-17; 1 Corinthians 12–13)

The apostolic attitude spontaneously chooses to work in a team or to travel in a pilgrim companionship. The leader trains the team to hold one another accountable in the context of a broader team covenant and even surrenders himself or herself to that covenant. This is not to say that oversight is irrelevant, but to say that it is intended to guard boundaries more than prescribe actions.

❖ Income responsibility, not budget dependency (Matthew 20:1-16; 1 Corinthians 2:1-16; 2 Corinthians 11:1-9)

The apostolic attitude takes responsibility for personal survival. It bakes its own bread and does not require that it be provided. Leaders are willing to work for a living and raise money for mission and are not dependent on a church salary and benefits or a budget line from a parent denomination. This is not to say that they will not gratefully accept the subsidy of a church or other institution, but to say that they will free themselves and the mission with which they are entrusted from dependence on anything other than the Holy Spirit.

The apostolic attitude is a requirement for *all* Christians. Both disciplined members and spiritual leaders (the two basic orders of ministry in the pagan world and the monastic model) must have it. This is not the unique attitude of bishops, parish clergy, or other professional experts, but the attitude of the Body of Christ as a whole. Of course, the public will never use the word "apostolic." They will, however, recognize preferential treatment of "the stranger" when they see it.

Apostolic Integrity

The second basic quality of spiritual leadership is integrity, but it is integrity of a unique kind. It is integrity that is shaped by the necessities of the mission field. It is the higher standard of integrity that is required for Christians who are generally despised to gain a hearing among pagans who are generally selfish. The public measures integrity differently than the church measures it. On the one hand, the public evaluates integrity based on the consistent, predictable, positive *behavior* of its spiritual leaders. The truth is revealed in the spontaneous deed and the unrehearsed word. The church, on the other hand, evaluates integrity based on professional practice. The strategic plan and the rehearsed word reveal the truth.

Public	Church
Behavior	Professional Practice
Motivation	Theological Knowledge

Similarly, the public, on the one hand, observes behavior and inquires into the *motivation* of the leaders. Where is their heart? What is their real purpose? What do they hope to achieve? They look into the eyes of the leaders and examine the budget of their organization. The church, on the other hand, monitors the *theology* of the leaders. Where is their head? Do they understand correctly? Have they mastered the theory? They listen to the tongue of the leader and examine the liturgy of worship.

Once again we see the striking parallel between the monastic movement that emerged as an alternative to the established church and the expectations of the seeking publics. It is precisely the behavior and motivation of the established priesthood that was questionable and the behavior and motivation of the monk or nun that was celebrated. The diocesan priests (like the denominational clergy today) organized their lives around an ecclesiastical polity. The monastic leaders (like the apostolic leaders today) organized their lives around a spiritual discipline.

Monastic Discipline	Diocesan Polity
Humilitas	Job Description
Conversatio	Dogmatic Exposition
Humanitas	Supportive Visitation

Monastic discipline demands the subjugation of one's entire life to the unpredictable experience of the Holy, a constant conversation with God and culture that leads to the overthrow of the devil, and compassionate service to "the stranger" in all his or her multiple needs. Diocesan polity demands the obedience of only part of one's life to the needs of the institution, a constant confrontation with culture based on an assumed certainty about God's will, and compassionate nurturing for the members of the church and their extended families. No doubt that rather stark contrast will seem unfair to the bishops and pastors within the diocesan polity, but unfortunately, that is how the SYiA and PCM publics see it.

In my previous writing, I have defined "integrity" as the shared core values, bedrock beliefs, motivating vision, and strategic mission that is the rhythm of life or the identity of the organization that is the church. This varies according to the unique culture and context of any particular church. Yet, there is a fundamental apostolic integrity that grounds every church with an apostolic attitude.

➤ Core Values (Galatians 5)

Apostolic integrity depends on the spontaneous and daring demonstration of the fruits of the Spirit. Spiritual leaders model and modify a peculiar behavior that markedly contrasts with the rest of culture, but also with the actual behavior of established churches. Among SYiA and PCM publics, it is the church (not society) that in reality models the desires of the flesh (fornication, impurity, licentiousness, idolatry, sorcery, enmity, strife, jealousy, anger, selfishness, dissension, party spirit, envy, drunkenness, carousing, and the like). It is all the more important for apostolic leaders to model the fruits of the Spirit (love, joy, peace, patience, kindness, goodness, faithfulness, gentleness, self-control) in the reality of which there is no need for polity.

➤ Bedrock Convictions (Colossians 1)

Apostolic integrity depends on Christocentric conviction. This is not as simple as it sounds, because the experience of Christ has multiple layers of meaning and significance. To paraphrase the Chalcedon confession, Jesus the Christ is fully human and fully divine, an infinite paradox that cannot be contained in any dogma or formula, which is crucial for the salvation and abundant life of all people and creation itself. The experience of Jesus the Christ can take many forms, and Christians may connect with Christ in different ways at different times, but "knowing Christ" in the ancient way of "merging with Christ" or "participating in the life, death and resurrection of Christ" (see Philippians 3:7-11) on a daily basis is the bedrock conviction of Christian integrity.

➤ Motivating Vision (2 Corinthians 4)

Apostolic vision depends on a "treasure" of supreme worth (which one might philosophically describe as "ultimate concern" or "absolute goodness"), which is even more unique because it is a person rather than a thing. It is a relationship that ennobles the human being and elevates human nature toward unity with the divine. More important, this is not just a future relationship, but a present relationship, which is actively and triumphantly empowering the apostolic agent toward every innovation and any sacrifice to share that treasure among the public.

Any number of metaphors can express this treasured relationship, but the imminent reality of this "treasure" drives the spiritual leader into mission.

➤ Strategic Mission (Acts 2:1-11)

Apostolic mission depends on the historical experience of the Spirit being heard in every language and by all cultures. The initial outpouring of the Spirit is strategically accomplished in a way that is relevant to every conceivable microculture in the world. That alone reveals that the subsequent strategy simply to stay in Jerusalem, or remain within the institutions of religion, is a flawed strategy and contrary to God's will. God intended from the first that good news should be shared with both "Jews and Gentiles." Apostolic mission focuses on anyone who is a "stranger to grace."

Apostolic integrity is a requirement for *all* Christians. It is part of the discipline of membership and the focus of leadership. Beyond this there may be many tactical innovations or doctrinal variations. However, the goal of apostolic leadership is *not* to synthesize theological perspectives into a systematic whole. The goal is to maintain this basic integrity at all costs, expelling those "members" who claim to be Christian and are not, and including those Christians who live in this integrity no matter how odd or different their culture, language, or lifestyle.

Apostolic Skills

The third basic quality of spiritual leadership has to do with skills, but the very word "skill" is defined differently in this context by the public. The church tends to assume that leadership skills are much like any other kind of skill. They can be taught to us. One can go to school or seminary and learn leadership skills in the same way as one learns preaching skills, writing skills, or counseling skills. Yet even corporate business has realized that leadership skill is categorically different from other skills. Leadership is an art. And the art of leadership is not trained. It is mentored. This is why apostolic succession in the earliest church was not achieved through the public education models we know today. It was achieved as handpicked disciples sat at the feet of mentors, shadowed their activities, observed their actions, absorbed their attitude, and received their wisdom. Apostolic skills are not learned in classrooms or seminary campuses, and they cannot be inculcated by a few weekends of "field work." The art of apostolic leadership comes through forms of apprenticing and small group dialogue at the feet of a mentor.

If one did not make this crucial distinction, it would be tempting to list apostolic skills in tactically limited ways: persuasive preaching, compelling teaching, and so on. Yet one of the most fundamental tenets of apostolic leadership is that no tactic is sacred. Tactics come and go as time and technologies pass. There are four fundamental apostolic arts mentored from one disciple to the next.

- Discerning between spirits (Acts 5:1-15)

> The gift itself is mentioned in 1 Corinthians 12:10 and is applied to the ability to distinguish Christ from the "elemental spirits of the universe" (Colossians 2:8). This perfect intuition only comes from a profound unity with Christ that allows the apostle to speak "in the Lord," and even then it is clear from Paul's experience that he himself feels the need to be very careful in separating his own ego from his authoritative voice.

The practical outcome is that the apostle can break through the essential ambiguity that pervades daily life and see the truth clearly. Discerning between spirits allows the apostolic leader to confront "control," and break the mission of the church free from dominating personalities or selfish egos. The confrontation with Ananias and Sapphira is revealing, not because they died as Peter confronted their attempt to control the church, but because there is no record that Peter felt guilty about it or that other Christians questioned it. The apostolic art is the recognized ability to penetrate to the truth of the matter.

• Connecting Christ with pagan cultures (Acts 17:15-34)

The art of apostolic leadership is the ability to empathize with any and all microcultures, simultaneously valuing their customs, insights, and religious practices and revealing the experience of Christ from their own midst. It is this ability that leads Paul to say that whenever Christians see truth, honor, justice, love, or anything excellent or worthy of praise, they should "think about these things" (Philippians 4:8).

The apostolic leader does not bring Christ to a pagan culture. He or she recognizes Christ within the pagan culture. Christ is already there. You know that because you see the telltale signs of the fruits of the Spirit. The task of the apostle is to get to know the culture so well that he or she can unveil the truth of Christ in crystal clarity as something the people have intuited but not fully understood.

• Readiness to risk martyrdom (Romans 14:8; Philippians 1:12-24)

The art of apostolic leadership is to face the reality—not the theory—of one's own death in absolute faith. The second millennium of the Christian era is really the story of a "Christianized" culture, in which martyrdom had become an extraordinary experience. In the first millennium, and now in the third millennium, martyrdom is once again becoming an ordinary experience. This sense of continually staking one's very life (and that of family, friends, and associates) on the relationship with Christ shocks the established church leader. Yet it is already emerging as an "ordinary" risk of Christian mission in most of the world; and in the next few decades it will even become a risk of daily living in Canada and the United States.

This is not a theoretical risk of martyrdom, nor is this presented as a values clarification exercise to help leaders uncover their life priorities. It is simple reality, and the imminent risk of martyrdom refines true faith with fire. How Christians face death reveals the truth about how they face life. The apostolic art is to model faith facing death, so that it reinforces their mentoring on how to live life. Martyrdom is the ultimate statement of what it means to be "in Christ." It reveals absolute trust, and absolute trust in life or death is the art of spiritual leadership.

• Anticipating the return of the Lord (2 Peter 3)

The art of apostolic leadership is the ability to hope and to instill hope in others. Defining or defending when, where, how, and what the coming of the Lord will look like has never been a preoccupation of spiritual leadership. Nor is their concern the loving harmony of God's people. The real concern is to help the church wait for salvation (including all the justice, peace, health, reunion, and other aspects of our deepest yearning). How do we endure? How can we persist? How can we keep going?

The art of spiritual leadership is to keep the promise alive. Despite the seeming victories of evil and suffering in the world, there is still hope. This is not shallow optimism, but a confidence borne out of a living relationship with the incarnate Christ. There is a thread of connection between the presence of Christ now and the coming of Christ in the future that cannot be broken. The apostolic leader keeps hope alive.

Once again it is apparent why such spiritual leadership is so precious to those outside the environment of the established church. SYiAs and PCMs gravitate to such leadership, just as the public gravitated to monastic leaders in the fourth through tenth centuries. Viewed from the outside, this is the practice of leadership most valued in a world living in fear of pandemics, corporate feudalism, and terrorist attacks.

Apostolic Teamwork

The fourth basic quality of spiritual leadership is the ability to surrender hierarchy to the mutual accountability of the pilgrim band. This is really demanded by the attitude, integrity, and art of leadership described above because without it the spiritual leader could easily become a dogmatic dictator. The difficulty is that the emerging pagan world has as much trouble understanding institutional Christendom as the ancient Celts, Magyars, and Vikings had understanding the hierarchies of the Roman Empire. Every church plant that begins with an apostolic team inevitably seems to end up (twenty years, five hundred additional members, and several specialized staff later) as some form of dictatorship. There is a direct connection between the decline of credibility for apostolic mission and the rise of hierarchy that replaces teamwork.

Teamwork is not about authority, but about influence. Therefore, when many ordination liturgies commission new clergy by saying "Take thou authority," at that very instant they begin to lose credibility among the public. The public does not just doubt that the church has the power to grant such authority, but it feels that that authority does not even begin to describe the essence of spiritual leadership.

Apostolic teamwork is founded on the ability of a spiritual leader to draw people into a sphere of influence shaped by the missional attitude, high integrity, and skillful action of the leader. The leader is seen as a mentor who can help—but not *control*— the personal growth and effective action of others. The leader is given credit as an "authentic" spiritual life and mission agent, and that credit is not "conferred" by an institution, but "earned" in the daily life, interaction, and visible sacrifices of the leader. The bonds of fraternity that hold a team together are not based on certification or even professional respect. They are held together by the authenticity of the leader. The fragile nature of a true team is revealed by the fact that authenticity that takes years to develop can actually be lost in an instant through an inadvertent action or injudicious word.

The experience of the team is even more complex, however, because spiritual leadership calls forth spiritual leaders. Like is attracted to like. It is not that others are drawn into a single sphere of influence, but that multiple spheres of influence merge or intersect. We read about Paul traveling with a pilgrim band that included, at various times, Luke, Timothy, Silas, Priscilla, Aquila, Onesimus, and others. These people were not empty shells when they were invited to join the team, but all had already established themselves as "spiritual leaders" in their own way. Each brought a "sphere of influence," so that the pilgrim band was really not a group of five people traveling within the aura of Paul's credibility, but six people (including Paul) traveling within overlapping auras of credibility.

This is the reason that the "falling out" between Paul and Barnabas over the inclusion of John Mark on the team was both so difficult to experience and so easy to solve (Acts 15:22-41). The problem was not that Paul doubted the spiritual leadership of Mark. The problem was that in the overlapping spheres of influence demanded of the apostolic team, Paul and Mark didn't "fit." They didn't converge. The team experience of the whole was not greater than the sum of the spheres of influence of each part. The solution was easy enough. Barnabas chose Mark, and they presumably traveled in their own distinct apostolic team, while Paul and Silas went their own way. Neither team was better than the other, just different. More important, both teams "worked."

There is a fluidity about apostolic teams that is not found in institutional hierarchies. In order to hire or fire staff, elect or reject volunteers, or call or dismiss clergy, there is always an inordinately long procedure to follow. Interviews take place, meetings are held, consultants are brought in, policies are reviewed, lawyers give advice, and months later a decision is made. How different it is in the apostolic team! Decisions are made overnight—or at least in a very short space of time—largely through the prayer and discernment of the team itself. No outside hierarchy intervenes. The team decides. And as a team of spiritual leaders, who are always growing and changing as led by the Spirit, the team is constantly adjusting and changing as team members come and go.

Here, then, is the full contrast between apostolic leadership and ecclesiastical leadership. It is remarkably parallel to the contrast between monk and priest in ancient times.

	Apostolic Team	Church Representative
Attitude:	Fundamental preference for the "stranger"	Fundamental preference for the "member"
Integrity:	Behavior Motivation	Professional Practice Theological Knowledge
Skills:	Discerning between spirits Connecting Christ and pagan cultures Risking martyrdom Anticipating the return of the Lord	Performing institutional tasks Correcting public error Risking status and advancement Preserving the harmony of the church
Teamwork:	Pilgrim Band Intersecting spheres of influence Fluidity	Salaried Staff Hierarchical authority Rigidity

Viewed from the outside, the apostolic team will always have more credibility than the church representative. Many clergy today are caught between these two incompatible expectations. In order to have credibility among the SYiA and PCM publics, they must function as an apostolic team. But in order to have job security and function within the system of ordination, they must function as church representatives. They are monks who are forced to be priests, or they are priests who are unwilling monks.

Orders of Ministry: Bishops, Priests, Pastors, Lay Preachers, Agencies, and Everything In Between

I have been arguing that, viewed from the outside, the public only really distinguishes two orders of ministry: spiritual leaders and disciplined disciples. Yet more can and should be said about how the pagan publics differentiate between spiritual leaders and their apprentices, and how this might influence future definitions of the orders of Christian ministry.

The emerging pagan world (like the ancient pagan world) values four spiritual roles for leadership. Some people may play multiple roles in their lifetime.

- **Priests:** The priests or priestesses address the spiritual hunger for supernatural experience. They stand at the intersection of the natural and spiritual worlds, helping individuals and community connect with God's grace or judgment. It is not just that they can "control" access to the divine, but that the divine "controls" them in order to connect with the world. A false priest is a mere magician. A true priest is a conduit to God.

  In Christian context, the spiritual leader as priest celebrates and shares the sacraments. The general public believes in sacraments. They believe that God can and will use ordinary things to reveal and share divine grace that will help people in the natural world survive and thrive. A false Christian priest is a mere preacher. A true Christian priest really believes in the real presence of Christ.

• **Oracles:** The oracle addresses the spiritual hunger for connection with the timeline of history. One could use ancient words such as "prophetess" or "seer," but these words are too laden with modern misunderstandings. The oracle deeply understands the significance of tribal history to the present moment but is able to see or predict how tribal history will come out in the future. A false oracle is a mere ideologue. A true oracle challenges human responsibility.

In Christian context, the spiritual leader as oracle ecstatically links past and future that is both judgment and promise for Christian disciples. This is not merely extrapolation of cause and effect, when so-called prophetic ministers simply draw out inevitable consequences from past actions. It is a more charismatic revelation of what God will do in response to human folly. A false Christian prophet is a wily bureaucrat. A true Christian oracle is a humble visionary.

• **Philosophers:** The philosopher (in a more ancient understanding of that word) addresses the spiritual hunger to "make sense" of life. He or she provides a reasonable interpretation of existence and advice for moral conduct. Each may have his or her unique point of view and form distinct and even incompatible schools of thought. Philosophers are always more interested in marketing than in any other role in spiritual leadership. A false philosopher is a sophist. A true philosopher reveals the significance behind mere words.

In Christian context, the spiritual leader as philosopher is a combination of coach, counselor, and teacher. Philosophers organize doctrine and religious practice into a purposeful whole that has practical implications for mission. They deal in theory that has a point and practical advice that has a foundation. A false Christian philosopher is a theologue. A true Christian philosopher is a theologian.

• **Ascetics:** The ascetic addresses the spiritual hunger for models of spiritual life. Their denial of not only luxuries, but even the seeming necessities and safety nets of life, pares away all distractions to reveal the essential spiritual discipline of living. The public imitates the ascetic not by duplication, but by approximation. They begin to focus, prioritize, and shape lifestyle around a clearer significance and meaning. The false ascetic is a freeloader. The true ascetic is an inspiration.

In Christian context, the spiritual leader as ascetic is likewise someone whose example of rigor and sacrifice reveals the essential "life of Jesus." Those who would come close to Jesus live like *this*. The more focused and self-disciplined you are, the more closely you participate in the life, suffering, death, and resurrection of Christ. The false Christian ascetic raves against consumerism but still relies on a salary and benefits. The true Christian ascetic takes responsibility for his or her own survival in order to merge work and spirituality.

These are the four basic roles of spiritual leadership that are valued in the pagan world. The temple priests of today's pagan world may be Internet gurus and New Age priestesses. The oracles today may be television talk show hosts, journalists, financial advisers, and environmentalists. The philosophers may be Hollywood stars or pop fiction authors. The ascetics may be fitness coaches and health food advocates. Yet all of these people have more credibility to the public as "spiritual leaders" than the average Christendom clergyperson has.

It is illuminating to observe what roles are *not* included in the list. First, "care giving" is not included in the list of credible roles for spiritual leadership. This is not to say that care giving is unimportant, but to say that it is something expected of *all* people and is not specially assigned to spiritual leaders. Also, "worship design" is not included in the list. Any entertainer, artist, or performer should be able to choreograph a meaningful venue for worship. Finally, "asset management" is not on the list. Any shrewd person of business should be able to maintain, invest, and develop the relatively meager budgets and properties of the church. The irony is that these three roles that are least credible for spiritual leadership among the public are precisely the three roles that occupy the most time and energy of the traditional clergy.

Although the common Judeo-Christian heritage can, and should, be preserved and celebrated, it is no accident the apostolic mission decidedly broke away from Jewish Christian communities (cf. Acts 18). In the same way, apostolic mission breaks away from established Christendom congregations that assimilate new members primarily through intermarriage, child rearing, or membership transfer and protect the identity and hope of a single group of people. Apostolic leaders focus on the growth of the mission, expanding the identity of the "chosen people" to include all cultures and traditions.

The Bishop and the Mission Field

Global missiology is the single most distinguishing feature of the Christian movement. In the context of apostolic ministry, the *role* of the leader is defined in *relationship to the mission field.*

There is no artificial separation of an "office" from a "missional purpose."

In the context of public expectations of credible spiritual leadership and apostolic goals for global mission, what is the role of a bishop from the perspective of the mission field? It is the very pragmatic role similar to that of a pastor of a multi-site ministry. If anyone earns the respect of the public as a bishop today, it will be neither the denominationally appointed overseer nor the megachurch pastor, but the pastor who successfully multiplies an identifiable congregation to operate from multiple sites to distinct microcultures. That is a bishop. It is the role of the pastor, expanded to embrace multiple locations and targeted ministries. The bishop is the mission leader in a larger sphere of outreach. To the extent that the growth of leaders, the management of assets, and the deployment of missionaries effects results in the mission field, then the bishop will function as a COO of the missionary endeavor. The missionary development process is precisely parallel to the congregational discipling process, in which people are changed, gifted, called, equipped, and sent.

Earlier I contrasted leadership expectations for Christian institutionalism with those of Christian movements. We can extrapolate from this the role of the ancient and postmodern bishop. This is a pastor who is already familiar with incarnational worship, the application of scripture to daily living, the development of servant leaders, and doing battle with those "elemental spirits of the universe." This pastor has expanded mission to multiple places and peoples. Now he or she needs to coach the unique worship and learning path of each growing congregation, by keeping them aligned to a clear Christology and by constantly equipping the local leadership for changing circumstances.

	Christian Institutionalism	Christian Movement
Pastor:	**Orderly** Worship	**Incarnational** Worship
	Exposited Scripture	**Analogous** Scripture
	Privileged Membership	**Servant** Discipleship
	Cultural Confrontation	**Spiritual** Confrontation
Bishop:	**Uniform** Worship	**Indigenous** Worship
	Common Curricula	**Customized** Learning
	Standardized Polity	**Clear** Christology
	Policy Development	**Constant** Equipping

These tasks contrast sharply with the expectations of a bishop in the age of Christendom. In that world, the bishop is elevated to oversight over churches *that he or she never planted and multiplied in the first place.* In fact, the supposed objectivity or differentiation between the bishop and the churches that he or she oversees is considered an advantage in the Christendom world to guard against favoritism. In the Christian movement, every church is a "favorite" child because the bishop-as-pastor is intimately connected with the birth, growth, and success of each church.

In the modern world, the preoccupations of the bishop involved the management of operational budgets, decision-making procedures, and personnel deployment. In the postmodern world of the Christian movement, the preoccupations of the bishop are returning to the priorities of ancient times: mission targets, christological alignment, and volunteer empowerment. The rest is better handled by the local pastor on each site of ministry, so that tactics can be speedily customized for every changing context.

The logical extension of the bishop's preoccupations in the Christendom world is the expansion of "mission by agency." More and more mission is actually accomplished by independent agencies that really have nothing intrinsically to do with worship, Christian development, or the accountability of a pilgrim band. They are separately incorporated, nonprofit extensions of the diocese. Originally, congregational vitality drove mission by agency, but today, mission by agency actually saps the strength out of congregational vitality. In the emerging Christian movement, the primary unit of mission is once again the congregation. The separately incorporated agency either stands or falls on its own and no longer will be subsidized by a diocese or supervised by a bishop. The bishop is interested not in agencies, but in missionally vital faith communities.

The Pastor and the Mission Unit

The "mission unit" is akin to what Christendom described as the "parish." A mission unit is a "missionally vital faith community." Strictly speaking in apostolic language, the combination of the words "missional" and "faith community" is redundant. Missiology lies at the heart of Christianity. To be "in faith" and to be "in mission" are virtually the same thing. I deliberately use redundant terminology, however, in order to drive the point home to traditional Christendom institutions. In the previous thousand years (roughly from 1054 through 1918),[2] the diocesan movement of the Christian church transformed the mission unit into a parish. The faith community became defined *ecclesiologically* by location, liturgy, and theology. The Body of Christ *in motion* has essentially stopped by the roadside, built a cathedral, and become the Body of Christ *in residence*.

The pastor is the leader of a larger and more complex pilgrim band. It is not surprising that early monasteries were founded by retirees who were former centurions in the Roman military, and their genius was interpreted by William Booth in founding the Salvation Army. There is a certain mobile urgency and assertiveness to the primary Christian mission unit because it is actually "taking the field" to confront evil and proclaim Christ. Christendom has given the militancy of the Christian movement a bad reputation because it became associated with the expansion of institutional and political power. Yet there is a clear militancy to the apostolic mission simply because the principalities and powers of evil were so concrete and immediate, and the good news of the gospel equally concrete and urgent.

Therefore, the one characteristic that makes a pastor stand out from among the faith community is his or her higher sense of *urgency*. When they proclaim that the "Kingdom is at hand" or that "salvation has come," they do so in the face of the enemy. It is not a ministry to consolidate gains already made, but a ministry that communicates with seekers and confronts evil. This sense of urgency is almost always missing in traditional church institutions. Pastors spend more energy guarding their days off, protecting their family privacy, visiting members for coffee, attending civic ceremonies, burying the dead, and interpreting theology. Certainly they know that injustices exist and tragedies happen, but fundamentally (ontologically) the "battle is over." The SYiA and PCM generations do not agree. For them the battle is still raging. They are afraid of being overwhelmed and destroyed, or of being misled and deceived, so that the last and best option to which all life leads is a lonely and noble death. That is the reason they will connect with a leader of a Christian mission unit that is compelled by a sense of urgency.

The previous chart contrasted the preoccupations of Christendom clergy with the compulsions of "Mission Movers."[3] The former kind of leader focuses on orderly worship, exposited theology, honoring the privileges of membership, and correcting culture. The Mission Mover focuses on incarnational worship, applying scripture to daily living by analogy, the multiplication and modeling of servant discipleship, and the more fundamental (ontological) confrontation with the principalities and powers of evil. They lead a mission unit that is a camaraderie of missionaries, and not a "parish" that is merely a fraternity house for the initiated.

The difference in leadership role can be seen in the contrast between the candidacy questions asked by the institutional church and the implicit questions asked by the SYiA and PCM publics.

SYiA and PCM Missional Questions	Institutional Candidacy Questions
Is (s)he associated with miracles?	Is he or she in general agreement with the polity?
Is (s)he urgent about mission?	Does he or she love the church?
Is (s)he living an authentic spiritual life?	Is he or she a good preacher?
Will (s)he stake her life and lifestyle on Christ?	Will he or she accept the salary package?

In order to lead the mission unit against seemingly impossible odds, pastors need to stand at the intersection between the infinite and the finite. It is not that they personally do miracles, but that miraculous victories of grace and breakthroughs of the Holy Spirit seem to be associated with their leadership. Their urgency is aligned with God's urgency.

Aside from the bishop and the mission field, and the pastor and the mission unit, the ministry is a fluid experience of opportunistic tactical deployments. There is no point to designating innumerable offices, or differentiating between various kinds of ministers, since ministry is being reinvented with every changing circumstance. Teams and team leaders are sent out from newly planted or established churches (mission units). Their targets will vary, and therefore their training will vary. Sometimes they will be led by this person, and sometimes by that person, according to the effectiveness of mission and the unpredictable movement of the Spirit.

What Makes Sense—and What Does Not Make Sense—about Ministry

I am writing specifically with a view from the outside, in order to describe what makes sense to the SYiA and PCM publics. If we extend the PCM category to include the many current church participants who are restless with the church as it is and even now are considering dropping out or reducing their participation, the publics that are "outside" the Christendom parish are vast compared to the remnant remaining on the "inside."

Authenticity, Not Certification

It makes perfect sense to the general publics that bishops and pastors should be spiritual leaders. They should be authentic in their spiritual lives, associated with miracles (in the broadest biblical sense of that word), and urgent about the good news of Christ. It does not make sense that this authenticity should be in any way subject to the certification of an institution. It really has nothing to do with a grade point average or the approval of a representative democracy, and it is not legitimized by a certificate that hangs on the wall. This may be true for dentists, doctors, and accountants, but it is not true for spiritual leaders. They will be recognized only by their spiritual fruit.

Authenticity begets authenticity. If there is any guarantee of the authenticity of a spiritual leader that the publics have not really met yet, it is that they are recommended by a spiritual authority that they are confident is authentic. A letter from a disciple of Peter is received with respect because the disciple has been endorsed or recommended by Peter. The authenticity of the pastor, at least initially, depends on the respect people have in the spiritual life of the bishop. If they do not respect the bishop, they will not accept the pastor, regardless of how many certificates the pastor hangs on the wall or what seniority the pastor has in the institution. The real problem with the credibility of pastors today is not that they may be professionally incompetent, but that they are not authentic and they are sent by a bishop whose spiritual authenticity is *also* questionable or unknown.

This is the reason the earliest church considered "apostolic succession" so important. The authenticity of the pastor depended on the authenticity of the bishop, and the authenticity of a bishop depended on the authenticity of her or his predecessor or mentor. We have allowed bureaucratic certification to replace apostolic succession and have experienced a decline in respect from the pagan publics in the mission field.

Mentoring Community, Not Seminary

It makes perfect sense to the general publics that bishops and pastors should emerge from a mentoring community. That is how authenticity is passed on from one generation to the next or from one leader to the next. It does not make sense that mentoring should be equated with core curricula, classroom experience, grade point averages, and graduation ceremonies. It is not that course work, disciplined study, or professional training are irrelevant to mentoring, but that mentoring is larger and more important than the total of these things.

All seminaries recognize the educational process as a mentoring experience. A view from the outside suggests, however, that most seminaries do not really act on this and that denominations routinely ignore it. The mentoring experience in seminary is *not* particularly profound, pervasive, or consistent. Most students report that serious mentoring about spiritual life and mission urgency is lacking. Most teachers demonstrate considerable interest in their subject matter, and in those students who are interested in that subject matter, but are otherwise uninvolved in any kind of 24/7 spiritual coaching with the students. That is reserved for field work, but most field placements "use" their students as cheap labor and spend little time mentoring their students in spiritual life and mission focus. Meanwhile, the denominations rarely inquire about the seminary perspective on the spiritual life and mission sensitivity of students and pay attention primarily to their academic success, practical competencies, and knowledge of polity.

What makes sense to the general publics is that the leaders in charge of spiritual formation should in fact be "spiritually formed." They should come to the congregation not as "companions on a spiritual journey," but as "leaders of a spiritual journey." They are not "wounded healers" with an emphasis on licking their own wounds in sympathy with the rest of the wounded. They are "healers" who have experienced healing and can forget themselves in order to heal others. They are not "theologians" who are still trying to clarify what they believe, but "missionaries" who are quite clear about Christ and can empower the church to share Christ with a seeking world. What makes sense to the general publics is that the pastor was a disciple among mentors and has come to mentor more disciples.

Apprenticeship, Not Probation

It makes perfect sense to the general publics that pastors should first be apprentices to other pastors. Before sending a fresh, new congregational leader to lead a small congregational mission unit in some distant part of the mission field, that new leader should have spent significant time training with a veteran pastor who is already successfully leading a mission unit. It does not make sense that apprenticing should be measured in weekends rather than in years, or that a newly ordained minister should immediately be sent on his or her own to the most challenging places in the mission field. Why send a novice where there will be little support, lots of challenges, and huge demands for mature leadership?

The notion of a probationary ordination, or a temporary assignment as a spiritual leader makes no sense to the general publics. If a spiritual leader is a spiritual leader, then ordain him or her and get it over with. If it is unclear that a person is a spiritual leader, then do not ordain that person. Apprentice them to someone, in some mission unit, so that he or she can be grown into spiritual leadership.

It also makes perfect sense to the general publics that pastors *should be required* to be apprentices. They know that the most arrogant and least competent leaders in any profession are often the most recent graduates of the university, seminary, or training program. They may want to fast-forward into responsible leadership, but any high-integrity organization will hold them back first to do effective apprenticing with a successful practitioner.

Ordination, Not Guaranteed Income

It makes perfect sense to the general publics that the spiritual leadership of the pastor should be recognized by some supernatural sign or symbolic rite. PCMs will have sufficient memory of the Old and New Testaments to know that God gives some sign or seal of approval whenever prophets, judges, kings, apostles, or priests are called forth. SYiAs may be alienated and suspicious of institutional religion, but they are convinced that a spiritual leader stands at the intersection of the infinite and the finite and that this should be recognized in some symbolic or visible way. Insofar as the spiritual leader "succeeds" to the authenticity of a spiritual mentor, it also makes perfect sense that the mentor should have some role in "naming" and "celebrating" the passing on of authenticity.

However, it does not make sense that the symbolic recognition of spiritual leadership should be limited to an ecclesiastical ritual or that ordination implies any particular responsibility or privilege in regard to the institution. The institution is a *tactic* of the Christian movement and not sacred in itself. Individuals are ordained into a *movement of the Spirit* but not into a *tactic* that may or may not effectively follow that movement. Indeed, the publics are highly skeptical of divided loyalties. If the minister is ordained into a *tactic*, how can he or she objectively critique the tactic in order to align it more effectively with the movement of the Spirit?

This skepticism comes to a head when the church announces that ordination should imply a "guaranteed income." That makes no sense at all to the general publics. In their view, the institutional church represents just one current in the vast ocean of the movement of the Spirit. There are countless ways God might call forth spiritual leaders to make disciples of Christ through the creation of communities of faith, and a guaranteed income does not have to be part of the plan. Indeed, it might be counterproductive to the plan. This is not to say that a pastor shouldn't receive an income from a church, but only that the income and the ordination do not mutually depend on each other. The income will be given for other reasons related to competency and context. This removes the temptation to enslave the spiritual leader through financial dependency and expands the opportunities for spiritual leaders to innovate using new tactics for the Christian movement.

Pastors, Not Categories of Pastors

It makes perfect sense that some spiritual leaders, recognized through ordination, should become pastors. These pastors will lead the Christian movement through that historically effective tactic known as the "local church." They may even plant them and multiply them and eventually become bishops. However, once you recognize that the institutional church as we know it is only one tactic in a larger Christian movement, and once you separate ordination from seminary certifications and guaranteed incomes, it makes no sense to bureaucratically distinguish different kinds and categories of pastors. A pastor is a pastor. The spiritual leader who forms and leads a local church may, in the course of the same career, be paid or unpaid, full time or part time, vested or unvested, according to the changing exigencies of the mission field. All that we really need to know is that they are authentic, mentored, and ordained.

The mission field of the first and third millenniums is too fluid for categories of ministry to make much sense. Even the attempts to give titles to church leadership in the New Testament are constantly ambiguous and generally follow cultural and community habits of secular organization. Categorization assumes stability in both culture and Spirit that is simply not there. More than this, it presumes an institutional control of the Christian movement that is frankly offensive to PCMs and SYiAs and possibly blasphemous as a hint of institutional idolatry.

"Categorization" is a means of "control." Organizational life in every sector is moving away from control. Categorization is a top-down way of determining in advance what an apprentice must study, how much money a leader deserves, what rights and privileges he or she can expect (or not expect), and what tactics are permitted or not permitted. Worse yet, categorization dulls the edge of mission purpose. It allows leaders to do the job with little result. What makes sense to the publics is that organizations sharpen the mission, provide basic boundaries, and turn leaders loose.

Calls, Not Assignments

It makes perfect sense to the general publics that spiritual leadership should be based on a spiritual calling. Spiritual leaders should feel an overwhelming compulsion or urgency to go to *somebody* in order to accomplish *something* in the *name of Jesus*. What does not make sense to the general publics is that this compulsion should be replaced by an *assignment* to send somebody to some place in order to do much the same thing other people might do in every other place. An appointment is not a call, and the simplest seeker knows it.

What worked well in the Christendom world does not work well in the pre- or post-Christendom world. Fluidity is the rule, not uniformity. Change is the norm, not continuity. Beyond the demographic, and beyond the lifestyle segment, there is an ever-expanding diversity of microcultures. Whether the paradigm is Jonah unwillingly going to Nineveh, or Paul joyfully going to Macedonia, the call is a compulsion to a particular people, to bring a particular experience of grace.

Call	*Assignment*
To a specific people;	To a specific place;
To pursue a special mission;	To maintain a church;
With profound urgency.	With a strong sense of duty.

An assignment is more concerned about the location of the ministry than about the people toward whom the ministry is targeted. It maintains continuity with the past, or stability of local tradition. It presumes a loyalty to an outside bureaucracy, which is stronger than love for a particular people. The call will be guided by the Spirit and certainly can be counseled by spiritual mentors; but in the end, if it is not an inner urgency generated by keen sensitivity to the mission field and the movement of the Spirit that drives a spiritual leader to embrace change, then it is not a call. The SYiA and PCM publics are not stupid. In five minutes of conversation at the front door of the church, they know if the pastor is there because he or she *loves them*, or if the pastor is there because he or she is loyal to the bureaucracy that sent him or her there.

Faith Communities, Not Agencies

It makes perfect sense to the general publics that the primary unit of mission is a faith community. This can be further defined from the New Testament as "two or three people gathered in Christ's name," or, in the history of the Christian mission, as the pilgrim band. Spiritual leaders never travel alone. For one thing, they are mentors who always travel with apprentices. For another thing, they are spiritual leaders in need of help constantly to distinguish between their personal desires and the will of the Lord. And finally, they are spiritual leaders who understand that they simply cannot carry the burdens, face the risks, and do the work *alone*. Spiritual leaders travel in good company.

What does not make sense to the public is that the church should do work through agencies. These may include various nonprofit health care groups and social services. Increasingly, however, the public can no longer distinguish between a local church and a local Lion's Club. Instinctively, the publics understand that a Christian movement has to be about Christ and faith, as much as about good works. It's about *disciples* working to multiply *disciples* (who probably will do all kinds of good works), but it is *not* about employees and institutional volunteers just doing lots of good works.

Faith Community	*Philanthropic Agency*
Mission to share Christ	Mission to do good
Faith formation	Social change
Personal transformation	Personal growth
Independent of government subsidy	Nonprofit with nontaxable benefits

It does not require a degree in philosophy to construct and apply the syllogism. All faith communities will become philanthropic agencies; but not all philanthropic agencies will be faith communities. Most local churches claim to be faith communities but are in fact philanthropic agencies. The publics may appreciate them because they do good things, are beneficial to society, and encourage personal growth and family development. Unfortunately, most churches require so much overhead to maintain useless space and employ staff to do irrelevant religious rites, that they are increasingly ineffective as philanthropic agencies.

This skepticism comes to a head when churches claim nontaxable benefits. It becomes apparent that the desire to qualify as a nonprofit corporation has nothing to do with philanthropic service and everything to do with obtaining hidden subsidies to maintain property and salary structures that are privileges of institutional religion. This is a pretense or a subterfuge that undermines credibility with the public. The public says:

If you are a philanthropic organization, then just be that, and stop trying to divert money to maintain useless religious paraphernalia. Reduce the overhead and give every penny to charity.

If you are a faith community, then just be that, *and stop trying to get government handouts from the taxation of people who don't care about your religion. If you love God, don't settle for giving 10 percent to God. Give it all.*

This extends to the spiritual leader. Nontaxable benefits in the salary package of clergy (housing and book allowances, freedom from property taxes, and so on) *reduce the credibility of the clergy as spiritual leaders.* It is a hidden subsidy that is offensive to the pagans, embarrassing to the believers, and demeaning to the clergy. It is a public acknowledgement that the church is unwilling to pay for spiritual leadership and that the clergy are in fact in debt to the secular government. Either God is enough, or God is not enough. Make up your mind.

Participation, Not Taxation

It makes perfect sense to the general publics that church members should take full responsibility to participate in the Christian movement. "Stewardship" is a funny name for it, but all organizations have their jargon. Participation clearly implies the totality of what we are and what we have, and not just a percentage. It's all God's, and if God lets us use 10 percent to buy groceries and take a vacation, that just proves how generous God is. But it's all God's. That makes sense to the PCM and SYiA publics. It is a contradiction in terms to believe in God and believe in private ownership. That's one practical reason that lots of people prefer not to believe in God. People who believe in God necessarily must believe in private *stewardship.*

Percentage giving as a measure of faithfulness does not make sense to the general publics, and the more the institutional church harps about it the less they respect the institutional church. Talk about money, by all means! That makes sense. But talk about *all* of the money and all of life and lifestyle, for that matter. Membership is an all-or-nothing commitment. The more members quibble over tax receipts and measure out their commitment in offering envelopes, the clearer it is that deep inside they harbor doubts about the value and efficiency of the church as a means of grace.

This skepticism comes to a head when the denomination demands a proportionate "tax" on the congregation to support judicatory infrastructures and agencies. PCMs and SYiAs know that the representational democracy that supposedly sets the annual "tax" is a sham. The "representatives" are not really "representative" of the congregation at all, but "represent" only a very small minority who are wholehearted in their conviction that the judicatory is an effective and efficient instrument of God's mission. What makes sense is that the congregation as the primary mission unit of the church should *participate* fully and completely in setting denominational budgets, policies, and priorities. The church cannot tax the congregation, on the one hand, and then impose policies and priorities that are not wholeheartedly supported by the congregation, on the other hand. *Stewardship* is about *wholeheartedness*.

Camaraderie, Not Fraternity

It makes perfect sense to the general publics that the clergy should feel a camaraderie, a unique bond of mutual support, that comes from experiencing the hardships and risks of a shared vision. They should sing songs such as "And Are We Yet Alive" whenever they gather together. It does not make sense to the publics that clergy should form a special club of the privileged few. They are not saints. The disciples are the saints. The clergy are the servants of the saints. In ancient perspective, the disciples are the soldiers and the clergy the centurions. The military language is used not to imply violence, but to imply peacekeeping. Together the soldiers and the centurions protect the boundaries of God's realm from the invasion of spiritual Huns and Vandals who seek to plunder and abuse and break God's peace that has been established through Christ's blood.

Therefore, the more clergy are distinguished from laity *by ecclesiastical office*, rather than *by missional function*, the more skeptical the publics become of the whole enterprise of the Christian movement. It is what fed the decadence of the Roman Empire, and it is what feeds the suspicion of decadence in the age of Christendom. Clergy spend way too much time staking their claims over preaching, sacraments, counseling, representation of the church in the community, and developing internal polity and far too little time equipping and training the "rank and file soldiers of the cross" for the Pax Divina of God's realm.

Like it or not, the general publics perceive clergy as a group to be an effete, outdated, ineffective club. As a class, they are reminiscent of the Drones Club in the satirical stories of P. G. Wodehouse. Of course, we know that it is not true. Not all clergy resemble Bertie Wooster dressed in a cassock alb (well meaning, self-absorbed, mildly amusing, and in need of the firm direction of Jeeves). Yet that is the *public perception* of the clergy. They are not going to give the clergy a raise based on a performance review counting all the pastoral visits, sermons, programs, and meetings. They look for a mission-driven leader who will equip the saints to establish God's peace, not the internal harmony and careless shenanigans of the Drones Club.

Accountability, Not Bureaucracy

It makes perfect sense to the general publics that all church leaders be held strictly accountable for their mission attitude, high integrity, continuous skills development, and ability to work in a team. That is the foundation of all credibility for leadership in any organization. What does not make sense is that the denomination rarely holds clergy accountable for these things. The denomination typically holds clergy accountable for bureaucratic performance: stable budget and property maintenance, preaching and "good worship" as defined by experts who are not practicing pastors, and keeping everybody happy inside the church. The public rarely sees the kind of accountability that leads to mission results. What they see is the kind of accountability that protects the appointment, apportionment, and appeasement expectations of the institution.

The skepticism of the PCM and SYiA publics goes deeper than this, however. This skewed focus of accountability would not happen if the congregational members did not want it to happen. The truth is that most active church members *want* it this way. They don't want to do a performance review of the pastor based on mission results, because that would necessitate a performance review of the church based on mission results. And the members are far too comfortable for that to happen.

This means that the primary oversight function of a bishop or judicatory leader should not be conflict resolution. All the money, time, and staff deployment among judicatories for conflict resolution actually reduces the respect of the general publics. The church sees a conflict among friends who need be reminded of their deeper love for one another. The public sees a brawl at the local bar that is only resolved when the pub owner mollifies the alcoholics with free drinks all around. The primary oversight function of a bishop is not conflict resolution, but control intervention. Both clergy and church members need to be held accountable for mission results simultaneously, and the codependency between clergy in need of authority, and laity who are all too willing to surrender responsibility, must end.

Multiple "Launching Pads," Not Redundant Properties

It makes perfect sense to the general publics that churches might own property. Any organizational leader who has ever rented space knows that you cannot allow a landlord to hold hostage the mission of that organization. You must control your own destiny. Not only might the organization own their own space, but they might own *many* spaces in order to target multiple publics. Clergy lose the respect of the general publics when either of two things happens.

Megachurches do not make sense to the general publics. It does not make sense to maximize overhead by building mammoth church campuses and expecting everybody to drive to them, especially when there are more traffic lights and higher gas prices. Yes, big box stores are successful, but only because there are *multiple* big box stores across the city. One big box per city is simply stupid.

Redundant properties do not make sense to the general publics. It does not make sense to maintain technologically outdated, or geographically marginalized, properties no matter how historic they might be. Preservation of architecture or art is a good thing, but it will only effectively be done by nonprofit heritage organizations. Community or neighborhood sustainability is a good thing, but it will only be effectively done by a state or municipal planning council. The church can't do it, and, more important, the church shouldn't do it. The more they cling to useless properties, the more they lose the respect of the general publics.

What earns the respect of the general publics is a readiness to buy, renovate, sell, relocate, or constantly upgrade property and technology to keep pace with the mission.

Mission Movement, Not Church Planting

It makes perfect sense to the general publics that church leaders should be constantly on the move. It does not make sense that church leaders should always yearn to settle down. Church planting is enormously popular today, but there are different kinds of church plants and different kinds of church planters.

This is what the publics do not respect. They do not respect bishops who insist all church plants must be led by certified, ordained clergy; be subsidized by judicatory funding; formally establish a constitution and bylaws before launching serious mission; and buy large acreages of land in order to erect an identifiably ecclesiastical edifice. They suspect that this "church plant" will grow up to be "just another church," despite all the rhetoric of the pastor and all the hype of the judicatory. And ninety-nine times out of one hundred they are right.

This is what the publics will respect. They will respect bishops who insist all church plants target a particular microculture with a peculiar experience of Christ; resource the *program* of the church but not the *salary* of the leader; permit anyone to lead who is willing to be held accountable to attitude, integrity, skills development, and teamwork; and subsidize communication technologies rather than the acquisition of land. Then the publics know that church leaders are serious about mission. And ninety-nine times out of one hundred they are right.

The Principles of Credibility

Historical precedent suggests that the restoration of clergy credibility will not come quickly or easily. How a culture treats its spiritual leaders, and how a culture views itself, are mirror images of each other. The clergy will not gain respect unless the culture gains self-respect; and the culture will not respect itself until the clergy deserve respect. It is not as simple as just providing better training, more performance reviews, positive marketing strategies, and clearer job descriptions. There is a *reason* the publics disrespect the clergy. They disrespect the clergy because deep in their hearts they suspect the church as a whole has conspired to deceive them. They believe the church has been forced into this conspiracy of deception because at root the experience of spiritual victory in Christ is false.

I have argued that PCMs and SYiAs represent stages of skepticism about faith, alienation from church, and disrespect toward clergy. They are all on the same road of doubt. One is just further along than the other. How are we to reverse the flow? The same categories by which the publics measure credibility reveal the essential principles through which credibility can be restored.

Attitude: The Principle of the Miraculous

A miracle is any "paradoxical blessing" that permanently changes the facts of life. The public expects spiritual leaders to be associated with miracles, and rightly so. Spiritual leaders stand at the intersection of the finite and the infinite. They point people toward a Higher Power, and they reveal to people divine grace. They are not part of the unbelief of culture. They are that rarity in culture of absolute belief *in spite of* all the evidence to the contrary.

Spiritual leaders have an attitude of expectation for miracles. These may be of various kinds. The biblical apostles were associated with ecstatic experiences of speech, healing, endurance, and discernment. The apostolic tradition associates spiritual leaders with sacramental experiences of the real presence of Christ in the Eucharist; the real transformation of the worst sinners in baptism; the real forgiveness of criminals in confession; the real calling of ordinary people to extraordinary things in confirmation and ordination; and the real hope of eternal life in unction. Even more than this, spiritual leaders are associated with "paradoxical blessings" that promise hope in any and all desperate situations in which inexorable fate seems to hold sway. They expect God to enter the room. They expect God to be there in worship. They expect God to change a heart.

The most fundamental way to restore the credibility of the clergy is to ordain only people who truly expect the miraculous, around whom paradoxical blessings seem to occur. The mission field does not need great preachers. Paul was not a great preacher. The mission field does not need great administrators or great educators or great diplomats or great fund-raisers. The apostles were barely competent in all of these roles. The mission field needs *miracles*. It needs spiritual leaders who are associated with miracles and who expect miracles. It is this "incarnational" experience that alerts the publics that the three great anxieties of fate and death, emptiness and meaninglessness, and guilt and condemnation truly can be overcome.

Integrity: The Principle of the Spiritual Life

The spiritual life is a 24/7 lifestyle of profound humility, disciplined personal growth, and radical compassion. All the various professional tactics we most commonly associate with ministry are largely irrelevant to the mission field. The credibility of the clergy does not depend on expertise. It depends on their ability to model virtue and align people to divine purpose.

Every authentic Christian reform movement in history has sought to restore the spiritual life to the center of Christian leadership. It is the heart of the monastic movement, the Gregorian reform, the Protestant Reformation, and all regional revivals such as the Methodist movement. The modern church has gone in exactly the wrong direction. The clergy look different from everybody else (with their collars, robes, vestments, and pious jewelry) but basically behave like everybody else. Exactly the opposite must take place. They must look like everybody else but behave differently from everybody else.

The higher standard to which clergy must be held accountable prioritizes core values (predictable positive behavior patterns) and bedrock convictions (faith principles to which they turn for strength in times of martyrdom). These values are revealed in their spontaneous deeds and unrehearsed words. These beliefs are revealed in the midst of their own stress, confusion, and pain. The public sees and believes.

Skills: The Principle of Effectiveness

Effectiveness can only be measured if the anticipated result is clear. That result is the multiplication of disciples of Jesus Christ. Effectiveness is measured by the legacy of people who have been transformed by the miraculous power of God and who have been equipped to follow Jesus into a mission that shares the miracle with the rest of the world. That is the "ends policy" of spiritual leadership. They do not need "procedural policies" or "denominational polities." Polity and procedure with no clarity about ends are not respected by the public. Clergy with no clear purpose are not *effective*; they are just *busy*.

Effectiveness is measured by the number of administrative meetings *missed*, by the amount of time spent *out of the church office*, by the *brevity* of the sermon, by the number of church members visited by *someone other* than the clergy, by the amount of learning accomplished *outside of the seminary*. The church cannot hold clergy accountable for effectiveness until it allows the public to hold the church accountable for effectiveness. The mission field, and not the church, dictates the priority of skills to be learned. The mission field, and not the church, determines the location, style of communication, and practical tactics of mission.

How can the clergy live in a culture of such intense spiritual yearning and desperation and yet fail to grow a church? How is that possible? The publics are dumbfounded. How can the Christian church be so ineffective? They must be unfamiliar with the power of God, unclear about their purpose, or unwilling to let go of privilege and risk discipleship. However, if they do let go of privilege and risk discipleship, and if they do expect miracles, and if they are clear about their purpose, then they will learn whatever they need to learn, and they *will* be effective. The harvest is just that plentiful!

Teamwork: The Principle of Companionship

Despite the individualism that dominates our culture, the publics do not respect leaders who can only work alone. The very mobility, changeability, and unpredictability of modern life feeds the skepticism that one person might know it all, do it all, or grow it all. The publics respect a team. Instinctively, they know there are three keys to credible companionship.

True companionship nurtures deep relationships. The publics respect clergy who can build effective leadership teams and nurture a deep sense of shared responsibility and mutual support across the congregation. It's not just "friendliness"; it's tough love, mission-driven unity, and the respect of a band of brothers and sisters who have endured much and accomplished more. It is a companionship that is worth more to God and to the mission field than the sum of its parts.

True companionship values adaptability. The publics respect clergy who know their limitations and can gather around themselves a team that can innovate, experiment, and adapt to the changing needs of the mission field. Why would they respect a preacher who has obviously run out of ideas, but who refuses to empower a layperson to take over who can speak God's Word more effectively in a unique context? Credibility increases as power to take initiative is given away.

True companionship practices constant accountability. The publics hold one another aligned to the higher purpose of the church and submissive to the miracles of grace. They hold one another accountable to the spiritual life of higher values and absolute convictions. And they hold one another accountable to the constant learning required to be effective in an ever-changing mission field. The credibility of clergy goes up the more they look for accountability within their own congregation, among their own leaders, and among the community networks most relevant to their context.

Overcoming the Church's Addiction to the Church

No prescription will work unless the patient decides to use it. After all the discussion, I return to the most basic issue. There is a fundamental assumption in the history of the Christian movement that alone protects the credibility of clergy:

> **The functions of church leadership are driven by the needs of the mission field, and not by the convenience of the institutional church.**

This principle has been systemically ignored for so long that the publics have lost respect for clergy, church, and, unfortunately, even Christ. It is because the church has become so arrogant in its theologies and so protective of its privileges and so defensive of its sacred cows that it cannot bring itself to take its own medicine of judgment and salvation.

The same existential anxieties that grip our culture grip the church. The lack of credibility of our spiritual leaders is just the mirror image of our lack of self-respect as a culture. Church and clergy have surrendered to the anxiety of fate and death, resigned to inevitable decline and even glory in self-righteous corporate suicide. They have surrendered to the anxiety of emptiness and meaninglessness, obsessing about empty buildings and career advancement. They have surrendered to the anxiety of guilt and condemnation, stressed into disability by feelings of inadequacy and judging one another more viciously than they confront the world. Why should the publics respect the clergy? They are no more faithful, no more hopeful, and no more loving than they are themselves, which is to say, in most instances, not at all.

The first step to credibility is not policy-making but courage. It is the same threefold courage that my mentor applied to the anxieties of our age.

✓ The courage of separation: Dissociate yourselves from the unbelief and immorality of our time. Model a spiritual life that is beyond question. Go monastic. Demonstrate integrity of purpose and a rigorous and single-minded alignment to imitate Christ and participate in Christ's mission.

✓ The courage of participation: Immerse yourselves in the world around us. Be sensitive to the demographics, lifestyle segments, microcultures, and affinity groups. Let your mission grow one heart burst at a time. Adapt the tactics, be incarnational, step out of your comfort zones, and do whatever it takes.

✓ The courage to accept acceptance: Open yourselves to miracles. Stand at the intersection of the infinite and the finite. Allow yourselves to be used or abused, deployed or set aside, raised high or laid low, as the Holy Spirit wills it to be. The Christian miracle is that the least credible people can become the most effective witnesses to grace.

There is hope for the restoration of credibility among the clergy, but it will not come easily. A glance back to previous historical crises makes this obvious. Our reform movement will be no less stressful than the birth of the monastic movement, the schisms caused by the Gregorian reform, the struggles of the Protestant Reformation, or the scorn and skepticism endured by the original Wesleyan movement. The stress is going to last for some time to come. Yet in the end a new, purified church will emerge. Spiritual leaders will once again work miracles, and Christ will bring welcome relief to billions of people on earth.

Notes

1. As defined by my mentor Paul Tillich in his classic post-war book *The Courage to Be* (New Haven: Yale University Press, 1952).

2. I date Christendom to have really begun with the inward turn of the church from the Great Schism that divided the western and eastern churches, and ended with the close of the First World War and the rejection of both aristocracy and theism in 1918.

3. See my book *Mission Mover* (Nashville: Abingdon Press, 2004).

CHAPTER TWO

A Faithful Response from the Inside

The mission field has changed. That fundamental fact has implications that are far more radical than the church has yet comprehended. Much has been written already about how the world has changed, and I will not repeat it here. Very little has been written about the remarkable lack of comprehension that has failed to translate knowledge into action. How can a church know what is going on and yet not *know* what is going on? How can the church persist in a basic public strategy of "just trust me" and fail to hear the public ask: "Why should I believe you?"

The Biblical Test for Credibility

The Gospel of John is all about accountability to Christ and Christ's mission. The earlier Synoptic Gospels are about the origin, history, message, and miracles that gave clues to the identity and purpose of Jesus. The Gospel of John was written significantly later, at a time when the Christian mission was already established and gaining legitimacy. John assumes the certainty of Jesus as the Christ. His worry is that the disciples be held rigorously accountable to the Great Commission. Accountability is the issue. If the other Gospels recorded the calling of the disciples, the Gospel of John hammers it home. There is no doubt that the disciples saw Jesus as the Lamb of God, or that they failed to see the implications of their agreement to follow him. There is doubt (at least at the time of writing John's Gospel) whether or not the disciples would remain true to the end.

Christian mission has become a "credibility issue" by the time John writes this Gospel. Christian missionaries are already being accused of immoral, antisocial, or deceptive behavior. Imitators are already distorting the Gospel and undermining public respect. The selfishness and immaturity of the Corinthians to which Paul refers in his letters are becoming all too normative. In John's Gospel time, the certainty and profundity of Jesus the Christ is a given. It is the faithfulness of his followers that is in question. Two stories in particular sharpen the call to discipleship.

The first story is unique to John. It is the story of the raising of Lazarus, and the first step in John's account of the journey toward the cross. It is usually understood as a definitive statement of the Lordship or saving power of Christ, but in fact it is really a story about the faithfulness (or lack of faithfulness) of the disciples.

> Now a certain man was ill, Lazarus of Bethany, the village of Mary and her sister Martha. . . . So the sisters sent a message to Jesus, "Lord, he whom you love is ill.". . . Then after this he said to the disciples, "Let us go to Judea again." The disciples said to him, "Rabbi, the Jews were just now trying to stone you, and are you going there again?" Jesus answered, "Are there not twelve hours of daylight? Those who walk during the day do not stumble, because they see the light of this world. But those who walk at night stumble, because the light is not in them.". . . Then Jesus told them plainly, "Lazarus is dead. For your sake I am glad I was not there, so that you may believe. But let us go to him." Thomas, who was called the Twin, said to his fellow disciples, "Let us also go, that we may die with him.". . .
>
> So they took away the stone. And Jesus looked upward and said, "Father, I thank you for having heard me. I knew that you always hear me, but I have said this for the sake of the crowd standing here, so that they may believe that you sent me." When he had said this, he cried with a loud voice, "Lazarus, come out!" The dead man came out, his hands and feet bound with strips of cloth, and his face wrapped in a cloth. Jesus said to them, "Unbind him, and let him go." (John 11:1, 3, 7-10, 14-16, 41-44)

Martyrdom—or the readiness to face martyrdom—became the ultimate standard of credibility in the earliest church. Even the public was impressed by the equanimity and piety of Christians in the arena. When Thomas says, "Let us also go, that we may die with him," he is articulating the commitment that lies at the core of credibility.

The problem is that Christian leaders today are at best ambivalent about what they think of Christ and certainly tentative in their readiness to make serious sacrifices for Christ's mission. They are skeptical that Jesus is doing the right thing by putting himself in harms way and doubtful that he can raise anyone from the dead. That, after all, would be just too miraculous. Belief is translated by church leaders into modern, scientific, therapeutic expectations. Faith becomes a metaphor for health. Belief becomes a metaphor for theology. Risk becomes a metaphor for ambiguity. The radical irrationality of faith, as Kierkegaard once so powerfully explained it, has gone missing from church leadership. And the public can sense it. "Why should we believe *you*," they say, "if you do not really believe *Christ*?"

All the great reformation movements in the past started with this simple, radical act of taking Christ at his word. Church leaders *really believe this stuff*. They are willing to stake their lives on it. Faith is not readily translatable, explainable, and controllable. The public knows this. They reasonably expect church leaders to know this.

The second story is also unique to the Gospel of John. This is the post-Resurrection story of Jesus meeting the disciples by the Sea of Tiberias. Remarkably, even after the death, resurrection, and mentoring of Jesus in the Upper Room, the disciples *still* did not know what to do!

> After these things Jesus showed himself again to the disciples by the Sea of Tiberias; and he showed himself in this way.

Gathered there together were Simon Peter, Thomas called the Twin, Nathanael of Cana in Galilee, the sons of Zebedee, and two others of his disciples. Simon Peter said to them, "I am going fishing." They said to him, "We will go with you." They went out and got into the boat, but that night they caught nothing.

Just after daybreak, Jesus stood on the beach; but the disciples did not know that it was Jesus. Jesus said to them, "Children, you have no fish, have you?" They answered him, "No." He said to them, "Cast the net to the right side of the boat, and you will find some." So they cast it, and now they were not able to haul it in because there were so many fish. That disciple whom Jesus loved said to Peter, "It is the Lord!" When Simon Peter heard that it was the Lord, he put on some clothes, for he was naked, and jumped into the sea. But the other disciples came in the boat, dragging the net full of fish, for they were not far from the land, only about a hundred yards off.

When they had gone ashore, they saw a charcoal fire there, with fish on it, and bread. Jesus said to them, "Bring some of the fish that you have just caught." So Simon Peter went aboard and hauled the net ashore, full of large fish, a hundred fifty-three of them; and though there were so many, the net was not torn. Jesus said to them, "Come and have breakfast." Now none of the disciples dared to ask him, "Who are you?" because they knew it was the Lord. Jesus came and took the bread and gave it to them, and did the same with the fish. This was now the third time that Jesus appeared to the disciples after he was raised from the dead.

When they had finished breakfast, Jesus said to Simon Peter, "Simon son of John, do you love me more than these?" He said to him, "Yes, Lord; you know that I love you." Jesus said to him, "Feed my lambs." A second time he said to him, "Simon son of John, do you love me?" He said to him, "Yes, Lord; you know that I love you." Jesus said to him, "Tend my sheep." He said to him the third time, "Simon son of John, do you love me?" Peter felt hurt because he said to him the third time, "Do you love me?" And he said to him, "Lord, you know everything; you know that I love you." Jesus said to him, "Feed my sheep. Very truly, I tell you, when you were younger, you used to fasten your own belt and to go wherever you wished. But when you grow old, you will stretch out your hands, and someone else will fasten a belt around you and take you where you do not wish to go." (John 21:1-18)

It becomes obvious what was holding back the disciples from mission. They simply did not have a clear priority for Christ and Christ alone. They were distracted, tempted, or addicted to other things:

- The old self—the former comfort zones, the former attitudes, the former obsession with self;

- The old life—the former activities, the former habits, the former relationships and privileges;

- The old career—the former job security, the former skills, the former standards of quality.

It is not an accident that the later apostles ranted continually about "being born again," "becoming a new creation," "dying to sin and living to Christ." They meant every word of it. Credibility depended on becoming a new creature and a new being. It was not a human achievement, but a result of meeting Jesus.

"Do you love me?" Jesus says three times. "Do you love me *more than these?*" Each time Peter's eyes are opened a little more. Finally, Peter gets it. He's supposed to love Jesus more than *anything*, even more than his spouse and family, dental plan, and retirement benefits, and even more than his self-confidence and his competence. In the context of the metaphor, Jesus is asking

Peter (and church leaders) if he intends to fish or cut bait. The public sees the church spending endless hours, and squandering enormous resources, sitting on the beach cutting bait. They expect the church actually to fish. In order to restore the credibility of the clergy, it is time for them to take the plunge.

Together, these two stories from John illustrate the two keys to clergy credibility then and now.

The first key to credibility is *unity*. Credibility depends on the solidarity of the disciple with Jesus. It depends on the transparency of one's obvious allegiance to Christ. Where Christ goes, I go, no matter what the risk. Indeed, Christ will almost certainly go where I do not want to go, yet I will still go. The experience of Christ is an indwelling unity with Christ. The disciple participates in the inner essence of the master; the spirit of the master penetrates to the very heart of the disciple. Jesus does impossible things; the disciples believe Jesus can do impossible things; they demonstrate to the public that if they participate in Christ they can do impossible things, too.

The second key to credibility is *urgency*. Credibility depends on the rigorous, even merciless, alignment with the mission of Christ. Nothing must sidetrack the spiritual leader from that mission, no matter how culturally acceptable or personally desirable that sidetrack might be. There is a reason Paul urged church leaders not to marry and the earliest mission teams urged churches not to buy property and build facilities. They were afraid that church leaders would get out of alignment with what was really important. They wanted church leaders to demonstrate by the ascetic rigor of their lives just how aligned the church really was to the mission of Christ.

Christendom tends to forget just how much the readiness for martyrdom was tied to the expectation of Christ's imminent return. Both are crucial to the credibility of church leaders who experience life as a daily risk and an urgent outreach. The problem with the credibility of clergy is that deep inside they always believe that they have more time. There will be time for more meetings and more strategic plans; time for a vacation or a day off; time for an academic degree program; time for a career to gain seniority; and time for the most resistant and selfish church member to figure it all out and get on board. The restoration of the credibility of the clergy also depends on the recognition that time is running out. Time is too precious. Get close to Jesus. Do it now.

Imminence and incarnation go together. The urgency of the "second coming" is tied to the reality of "already here." Unity with Christ leads to the passion to share Christ's mission, and participation in Christ's mission deepens unity with Christ. Mission aligns with Christ; Christ targets mission. The more the public sees a spiritual leader sidetracked, immobile, and dithering in meetings, obsessed by trivialities, or attending only to the ninety-nine sheep that stayed in the flock, the less respect they give that leader. The more the public sees a spiritual leader focused, active, reaching out to strangers, clear about priorities, and rescuing the one sheep that got away, the more respect they have for that leader. That is the leader who, through urgent mission, makes Christ incarnate in the world. They no longer "see" the church leader. They "see" Jesus.

Religion and Leadership in an Authentic Church

The publics have unique perceptions and expectations of both religion and spiritual leadership. In the first section of this book I tried to outline the key questions that PCMs and SYiAs bring to both matters. The lack of credibility among clergy is partially the result of trying to answer questions that, quite frankly, no one is really asking. It is not just their irrelevance that annoys the public. They suspect that the clergy are deliberately not listening. Therefore, the way to regain credibility is to start listening to their questions and providing answers to their issues about religion and leadership.

Plainly speaking, an "authentic" church is simply a church that provides answers to the actual questions people ask. These questions emerge from the three fundamental anxieties of their lives:

- the anxiety of fate and death;

- the anxiety of meaninglessness and emptiness;

- the anxiety of guilt and condemnation.

Everything an authentic church does, and an authentic church leader says, should be aimed at responding to these anxieties. Nuance is everything. Every microculture, and indeed every individual, has its unique perspective on or experience with these anxieties. Yet every microculture also refuses to face these anxieties directly and so seeks to sidetrack the church and spiritual leaders into other issues, conversations, and preoccupations. The inauthentic church allows this to happen because church leaders themselves are not united to Christ profoundly enough to have any answers themselves. The authentic church "cuts to the chase." These leaders refuse to be sidetracked and focus on the core human predicament and the fundamental divine grace.

There are two intersecting polarities or continuums that shape the authenticity or lack of authenticity of religion, and the credibility or lack of credibility of church leaders.

The Body in Residence and the Body in Motion

In previous writings, I have spoken of the ancient and postmodern dilemma of Christian religion as a tension between institution and movement.[1] The dilemma is first described in the first fifteen chapters of the Acts of the Apostles. Jesus sends the disciples to "go forth" in a movement that quickly became known as "The Way," but the disciples initially "retreated" to the Upper Room and the Jerusalem temple to institutionalize the church. Rather than go to the publics, they expected the publics to come to them. They believed they could stay in one place; borrow, rent, or own property; appoint greeters and church officers; develop a radical stewardship program; celebrate blended contemporary worship that would unite the best of the synagogue and the best of Greek culture; and settle down in a harmony of membership privileges.

One would think that the experience of Pentecost, in which the disciples spoke in every international language of the known world, might have suggested to the church that it should go out to those nations. In fact it takes an additional outpouring of the Holy Spirit, often experienced as quite stressful by Peter, James (the brother of Jesus), and the Jerusalem church, to convince them that they are following the wrong strategic plan. It takes Phillip, Paul, and a host of lesser-known missionary activists (male and female) to convince them to adopt the new strategy known as the "mission to the gentiles." The decisive break is described in Acts 18, as Paul dramatically leaves the religious establishment (the synagogue in his day, and the established church in ours) to relocate literally next door in the home of a gentile named Titius Justus. In spite of the fact that the church had been accused of watering down "good worship," the Holy Spirit confirmed that the only good worship is that which helps people answer their fundamental anxieties about existence with the incarnate or immanent experience of Christ.

This is a credibility issue. Paul is extraordinarily sensitive to Peter's dithering about protecting sacred customs or transforming desperate lives. The public are beginning to scoff. Is the church about salvation, or is the church about preservation? Paul criticizes Peter on several occasions precisely because he can't seem to realize the authenticity issue that is at stake. If preservation is what really matters, then the church will solidify again around structures; but if transformation is what really matters, then the church must liquefy to become as adaptable and creative as possible to reach people with the gospel. In a fluid world, solids are not credible. The church must be more like water than stone.

Obviously this dilemma about religion is as relevant today as in ancient times. When most people think of "church," they immediately think of ecclesiastical buildings, bench-like seating, sacred rites, exclusive membership, and so on. And as soon as they make this association, their hearts sink, their imaginations deflate, their tempers rise, and their frustrations grow. This is not the only way one can think of the church. It could be considered to be a movement, a way, a spirit, an attitude, and so on. This will make hearts soar, imaginations explode, joy increase, and interest grow. This is the Body of Christ *in motion.*

The Body *in Residence*	**The Body *in Motion***
Continuity	Adaptability
Predictability	Creativity
Uniformity	Diversity

The polarity or continuum of authenticity is thus really defined by proximity or distance from what I described earlier as the four *P*s of religion: property, program, personnel, and polity. The more obsessed the church is with these four things, the more it becomes the Body of Christ *in residence.* The more distant the church can become from these four things, the more it becomes the Body of Christ *in motion.* The residential nature of the church maintaining the four *P*s reveals the very essence of institutionalization that the publics find inauthentic. The true spiritual nature of the church as a transforming power for good in the world is revealed by its ability to adapt, create, and diversify.

Is it possible to do anything at all without using physical objects, implementing strategies, equipping people, or measuring accountability? No. But that is not the source of the public's incredulity when it comes to Christian religion. What they do not respect is the assumption that only certain kinds of objects, strategies, offices, and policies will suffice to make Christ incarnate and immanent. The Body of Christ in motion is only interested in objects that point to Christ, strategies that yield experience of Christ, leaders who mentor Christ, and accountability direct to Christ. Anything less is mere religion.

The Diocesan Leader and the Monastic Leader

If the first polarity or continuum shapes the authenticity or lack of authenticity of religion, the second shapes the credibility or lack of credibility of spiritual leadership. This also has its roots in history, but it is the history of the first millennium rather than of the apostolic age itself. Just as the mission to the gentiles began to solidify into institutional parishes and patriarchates, so also spiritual leadership began to legalize into offices and ordinations. Hierarchies, territories, authorities, and certifications began to replace the earlier teamwork, mobile spirituality, mentoring, and spiritual blessings of the Christian movement.

The diocesan leader is a political appointment first and a spiritual leader second. This statement is intended not to denigrate politics, but to recognize the importance of policy makers, administrators, and statesman in both the history of civil service and the history of ecclesiastical service. The process of borrowing Roman practices for administration reached its zenith when Christianity became the official religion of the empire, and thereafter clergy (pastors and bishops) were expected to assist civil government (and sometimes represent civil government) in the maintenance of good order. Christendom extends the maintenance of good order to the maintenance of "good worship," "correct theology," "proper procedure," "membership privileges," and everything suitable for the maintenance and expansion of the church institution. The diocesan leader (pastor and bishop) may *also* be a spiritual leader, but his or her office does not really depend upon that. It depends upon one's effectiveness as a political appointment that governs and guides the greater good of the church.

Early heresies such as Montanism and Arianism were not primarily disagreements in theology, and their bitter persecution was not primarily motivated by a desire to protect the saving nature of Christ. These movements were early challenges to the role of the diocesan leader as a political appointment. Montanists argued for a purely spiritual anointing of prophets and prophetesses revealed through experiences of visions and ecstasies. The epicenter of the movement in the mountains of Asia Minor was far distant from the imperial courts. Arians argued for greater distance between pastor or bishop and civil authority. Ironically, Arians accomplished more outreach among the barbarians of the west than orthodox missionaries who were carefully screened and trained by Rome.

I think an argument can be made that the later Protestant Reformation, and even later regional reformations like that of Methodism, was a similar reaction to the emergence of the diocesan leader as the standard Christendom clergyperson. Mediators such as Erasmus tried to convince both sides that a leader could be *both* spiritual *and* political at the same time, but it could only be true in a remarkably stable world of slow change, deliberate thinking, and fundamental trust in the system. Lose that—and the world then and now has lost that—and Christians are forced to make a daily either/or choice.

The monastic leader emerged from the same discomfort with diocesan politics. Unlike Montanist reliance on the uncertain and unpredictable authority of Spirit, monastic leaders based authority on radical submission to Christ. Like the earliest letters of Paul, their original thinking was probably more binitarian than trinitarian. Monastic life was based on:

- The Model of Jesus (Mark 4:12; Acts 16);

- Commission from Jesus (Matthew 28:18-19; Acts 8:26-40);

- Companionship with Jesus (John 21:15-19; Philippians 3:7-11).

Monastic leaders were primarily spiritual leaders, and not political appointments. Their credibility and following emerged from their ability to model the life, death, and resurrection of Christ in their personal living; and to apply to radical extremes the commission of Christ to rescue the world from sin; and from their almost erotic desire to unite with Jesus in complete companionship.

Therefore, the monastic leader is not preoccupied with good worship, correct theology, proper procedure, or membership privileges. The leader is preoccupied with:

❖ **Desire for God:** The passion to go *very* deep, and confront evil;

❖ **Unity with God:** The patience and courage to achieve profound self-knowledge and self-purification;

❖ **True Asceticism:** A lifestyle reorientation to transform the self and model right relationships;

❖ **Leadership:** The goal to demonstrate faithfulness by example, modeling, and mentoring.

Evagrius's path to knowledge, for example, was a journey from the recognition of God to the internal participation of God in every aspect of thought and living. Contemplation confronted and overcame all desires and fears; self-discipline aligned behavior to the model of Christ; charity and compassion merged with Christ's ongoing mission.

Diocesan leadership busies itself with the duties of office and the responsibilities of the institutional church. In other words, diocesan leaders are forced to manage their time. They are preparing sermons; visiting members; teaching catechisms; attending meetings; reading reports; supervising the installation of works of art and maintenance of sacred space; developing programs; choosing and supervising volunteers; and arbitrating disputes. They make sure that unworthy people do not receive the benefits of the church, and that worthy people always receive the benefits of the church. They will make time for personal prayers, devotions, meditations, and Bible reading *in the context of a busy ecclesiastical life.* That, in fact, is the dominant legacy of the church in the second millennium. Many reform movements have sought to shape it, control it, alter it, and redirect it; but the basic expectation of diocesan leadership remains constant.

Monastic leadership busies itself with precisely the opposite. Monastic leaders do not manage time. They surrender to the "right time." They are masters at expectant waiting, and they are aggressive entrepreneurs who can seize the moment when the time is right. Monastic leaders shape daily life around:

➤ Constant meditation on scripture: They copy manuscripts, cherish every word, and apply the scriptures to life *by analogy* so that every word is pregnant with meaning.

> Constant worship: Singing or psalmody is most important because worship is essentially a poetry of the heart that is constantly celebrating and praising God. They can sing to themselves or sing aloud, worship alone in a cell, together in a body, or in the midst of public chaos.

> Manual labor: Christian life permeates all life, and holy work merges with ordinary work. There is no *necessity* to be in a church to be close to God, when one can be close to God irrigating a field, making beer, or performing any chore. One can do anything *in a godly way.*

> Faith-motivated service: The seamless unity of the incarnation and immanence of Christ means that contemplation flows naturally into service to others, particularly to strangers, the sick, the defenseless, the hungry, and other outsiders generally ignored by the diocesan preoccupation with membership privileges.

Monastic leadership is not about church business, but about spiritual life. Diocesan leaders are apt to describe their routine in reference to Holy Days and career paths. Monastic leaders are apt to describe their routine as an endless flow of *humilitas, conversatio,* and *humanitas.*

This second polarity or continuum of credibility is thus really defined by proximity or distance from what I described earlier as the three *A*s of leadership: appointment, apportionment, and appeasement.

✓ The closer leaders are to the diocesan model of leadership, the more preoccupied they will be in protecting and promoting their own careers and the advancement of others. They will be extremely anxious about the financial income that can be expected to accumulate within the general budget for the pastor's salary and the denomination's infrastructure. They will be eagerly attentive to the harmony, agreement, and numerical growth of church members who pay the bills and influence the institutional measurement of success.

✓ The closer leaders are to the monastic model of leadership, the more preoccupied they will be with the spiritual life, outreach to the world, and the struggle between God and evil. They will be extremely anxious about unity with Christ and self-discipline. They will be eagerly attentive to alignment with God's will and participation in God's mission regardless of the conflict or resistance they might meet from the church.

The ultimate skill of diocesan leaders is conflict resolution. They must preserve unity today and continuity between the past and the future. The ultimate skill of monastic leaders is control intervention. They must oppose any effort to limit or contain the gospel, and they must battle with evil in its metaphysical and historical forms.

The following diagram uses the two polarities or continuums to describe how the church is, and how it might be. It helps church leaders of all kinds understand the distinct assumptions about religion and leadership in any given church and identify the next steps to restore the authenticity of the church and the credibility of church leaders.

The arrows indicate the direction of transformation. In the second millennium of Christendom (AD 1000–1999), the arrows were reversed. Indeed, the second quadrant of the diagram, which was once the leading edge of the first-millennium church, all but disappeared. Today, the majority of churches are the establishment churches; seminary enrollment is declining; and while charitable agencies are exploding, they are also leaving the church.

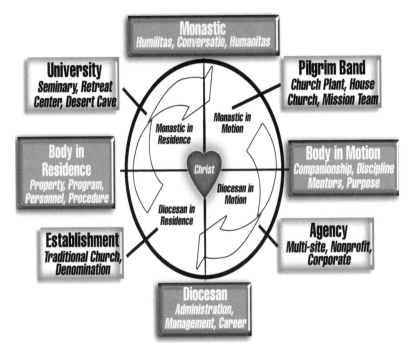

The leading edge of the Christian movement, and the quadrant of highest credibility among the public, is the pilgrim band. This has always been the case. These are the traveling monks of ancient time who have left their home countries, familiar surroundings, and liturgical spaces to take the gospel to the world. This is "monastic in motion"—monastic leaders who establish authentic faith communities. They resemble the Irish peregrines and Byzantine mendicants who carried the faith to the barbarians. Their initiatives may take various forms, including newly planted faith communities, house churches, and mission teams that target particular microcultures with innovative tactics.

The key word for "monastic in residence" is "university," but I mean this more in the original medieval sense than in the modern sense. The original "university" emerged from the monastic movement as an effort to preserve and expand learning. The love of learning and the desire for God were the same because "truth" was understood as a participation of the finite and the infinite. The practical experience of the university involved personal mentoring, disciplined reflection, and innovative experimentation; but it was all undertaken with a larger purpose of mission. Today's university typically separates reason from truth for a larger purpose of self-interest. It's all about professional training and scientific verification, segmenting the world into empirical databytes to be manipulated or consumed. The original university was all about discerning destiny and unity with the Spirit, uniting the visible and invisible realities in a larger synthesis of meaning. The goal was faith, not skepticism.

There are larger issues at stake, but my purpose here is to restore clergy credibility. In order to do that, there must be a reawakening of the dynamic connection between the university and the pilgrim band. Currently the relationship goes the other way. The seminary primarily serves and protects the establishment church, and their symbiotic relationship has encouraged the perception of clergy irrelevancy among the public. From the point of view of the skeptical public, the university (seminary) trains people to pontificate, procrastinate, manage tax-exempt property, and judge other people. The establishment church subsidizes the seminary and protects tenured faculty to provide that training. As Christendom disappears, both established church clergy rosters and seminary enrollments suffer.

The solution is not to discard the seminary, but to connect the university with the body in motion. The university can train leaders for the pilgrim band rather than the establishment church. Some are already trying, but the shift remains undersupported. The university can train apostolic leaders with the mission attitude, profound integrity, relevant skills, and teamwork abilities that the publics respect. This will involve a dramatic change to expectations for tenure, core curriculum design, faculty–student relations, and expanded field work and apprenticing practices. However, the greatest change that can increase the credibility of the clergy is to reverse the trend that defines the purpose of the seminary as being to train theologians. The establishment church wants theologians. The pilgrim band needs missionaries. The seminary needs to focus on empowering leaders for Christian mission, rather than assisting spiritual dilettantes to discover themselves. Seminaries can contribute to the credibility of clergy if they stop endless deconstruction and start serious faith formation.

The perception of the public is decidedly against diocesan leadership, but this does not mean that diocesan leadership cannot be faithful. No one is saying that the only way to lead is by becoming monastic. It is possible for the diocesan leader to be part of the body in motion. These tend to be agencies of social service and faith witness—hospitals, social services, nonprofits, muti-site churches, and corporations with an intentional missional purpose. The organizational structure is flexible. It may be a limited liability corporation, or an S-Corp, or a nonprofit with a board. The point is that they are in motion. They are competitive and, therefore, entrepreneurial. They are constantly adapting and changing with the times. The leaders may well owe allegiance to denominational appointments or ecclesiastical regulations, but they subjugate these to the great good of the peculiar mission of the agency.

The realm of least credibility is the "diocesan leader in residence." Unfortunately, this describes the vast majority of existing churches—evangelical or mainstream, independent or denominational. They are "the establishment." They are inextricably bound to civil religion and are integrated with the community socialization process that is valued by the state. They help the crime rate decline and family values grow. They preserve architectural and cultural heritages. They pray for graduating seniors and celebrate the sacrifice of military veterans. They dialogue about interfaith issues and seek out lowest common denominators to resolve historic denominational disagreements. They prioritize social justice and sacrifice faith witness in order to do it. They romanticize the family and idealize cultural diversity. They hobble the clergy by the almighty goal of membership harmony.

Ironically, the public both desires this and disrespects this. They want religion and religious leaders to benignly entertain and comfort them and powerfully to motivate them to go home to lunch. They want religion and religious leaders to tell them how to vote and what causes are worth slaughtering sacred lifestyles for, but in the end the public does not respect religious leaders. The pubic all for human progress, but in an age of addiction and original sin, they are profoundly doubtful about progress. They are beset by the three existential anxieties that neither public policy nor psychological therapy can address.

In the view of the critical publics, the "diocesan in residence" is the dinosaur of the twenty-first century. It is already dead, but sustained by bequests. In the view of the faithful church, it is in drastic need of reform and redirection. Together the pilgrim band, the university, and the agency will set about revolutionizing and reforming it.

At the center of it all is the experience of Christ. This is not the knowledge of Christ, nor the definition or dogmatization of Christ. It is the experience of Christ that addresses the three fundamental anxieties of the public. Somehow Christ reassures the crisis of inevitable fate and death with his impossible resurrection. Somehow Christ resolves the crisis of emptiness and meaninglessness with his companionship and purpose. Somehow Christ overcomes the crisis of guilt and condemnation with his radical forgiveness and acceptance. This is what seminaries should teach. This is what Christian agencies should implement. And this is what the pilgrim band proclaims.

Making Uncommon Sense

The publics are not looking for common sense. Indeed, the SYiAs and PCMs have largely surrendered their confidence in common sense. They are looking to the apocalyptic. They are getting ready for radical revolution. They are intuiting a solution to the human and global dilemma that is beyond strategic planning and scientific discovery. Yes, they are looking to make sense of the situation. No, they are not looking to find solutions within the accepted parameters of social reform. They are looking, paradoxically, for a concretely hopeful resolution to the existential condition in a nonrational experience of the Holy. In other words, they are looking for incarnation as a solution to the human condition, and they are hoping for immanence as a response to their longing. "Please," they say. "Make uncommon sense!"

The path to clergy credibility is a straight line from the experience of Jesus to the mission of Christ. Any deviation from this path diminishes the credibility of the clergy.

> ➤ Step to one side of this path, and confuse or complicate the experience of Jesus with abstractions, qualifications, and speculations, and the public no longer wants to talk with you. Your conversations will reduce to mind-numbing debate among ecumenical colleagues and theoretical discussion about the philosophy of religion. You will waste all your time trying to rationally explain what the Chalcedon Confession declared an inevitable paradox, namely, that Jesus the Christ is fully human and fully divine and that our salvation lies in the experience of that

conundrum. The gospel will lose its existential power and essential significance. The clergy will lose relevance, preaching a message of morality or mysticism that is not really that distinct from the other great religions of the world.

➤ Step to the other side of this path, and redirect or set conditions on the mission of Christ, and the public will no longer need you. Your work will reduce to philanthropic fund-raising and social service, the success of which depends more on who holds political office than on the power of God. You will waste your time in meetings managing a receding ecclesiastical empire or refining and marketing public policy like any lobbyist on Capitol Hill. The gospel will lose its infinite promise, and its expectation of judgment will be dulled by its association with lawyers. The clergy will lose relevance, offering a service that can be better done by other professionals or offering worship services that fail to attract the interest of other professionals.

The point is that today, as in ancient times, the credibility of clergy depends on one simple thing: the experience and mission of Christ. This is the continuum of "life in the Spirit." On the one hand, the mission of Christ depends on the experience of Jesus. It is meaningless without the incarnation. The more the incarnation is denied, obscured, or ignored, then the more the mission is irrelevant, ineffective, or easily rejected. On the other hand, the experience of Jesus is worthless without the mission of Christ. The mission fulfills the whole point of incarnation. The more the mission is deflected from its original purpose to make disciples of all nations, the more historically irrelevant and meaningless the experience of Jesus becomes. Credibility depends on the rigor with which clergy "walk the line" that begins with Jesus and ends in mission to the world.

Imagine for a moment how the mission to the gentiles would have looked if Paul had not declared simply that he preached "Christ crucified," a scandal to custom and an offense to authority (1 Corinthians 1:23). What kind of credibility would it have had if Paul had not declared that all he really wanted was to be with Christ, to share in his sufferings, and participate in his resurrection (Philippians 3:7-8)? What if Paul in Athens had simply delivered a philosophical treatise on essence and existence, and the metaphorical relevance of the cross for the principle of inclusiveness in a cross-cultural world? The hope of Christ would have shifted from the workplace to the coffee shop and eventually been lost in a sea of Gnosticism (which is exactly what is happening today). What if Lydia had obtained nonprofit tax exemption for the house church in Philippi, opened a street ministry that carefully avoided talking about Jesus, and developed a think tank to give the emperor unwanted advice on how to administrate Rome? The Christian mission would have shifted from daily behavior to weekly meetings and eventually would have been lost in the chaos of politics (which is exactly what is happening today).

It makes sense that any organization should ruthlessly align itself with its strategic purpose, and resist every temptation to stray from it. When Ananias and Sapphira attempted to deflect the church from the absolute claim of Christ over all of our life and lifestyle, to the *relative* claim of Christ over part of our life and lifestyle, Peter confronted them immediately and unequivocally. Ananias died, Sapphira grieved, and there is no record that Peter ever felt guilty about it. That single action probably rescued the earliest church from stepping off the path of credibility. If Peter had excused their behavior, fearful of losing a member of the church, or if Peter had formed an ad hoc committee to investigate the circumstances and make recommendations to clarify the constitution and bylaws of the fledgling church, then the Christian mission would have been reduced to yet another Jewish sect and never reached Philippi in the first place. The Romans could have ignored the Christian apostles as ineffective oddballs with a weird sense of priorities.

What is obvious for any organization becomes more radical for Christian organization. The incarnation is paradoxical, and therefore the Christian mission succeeds in doing the impossible. Who could imagine that the Christian church would transform the Roman world and eventually the entire globe? Who could imagine even today that the Christian movement—underfunded and led primarily by amateurs and clergy who are little better than amateurs—would overcome so many obstacles of war, plague, famine, prejudice, and indifference to become such an influence in the lives of so many people? It is nothing else but miraculous, just as the experience of Jesus is nothing less than miraculous. There is something more here than just professional preaching, acute church administration, and sensitive Christian marketing. It is the action of the Holy Spirit, and clergy stray from that power at their peril. Christian organization requires more than common sense. It requires uncommon sense.

Uncommon sense would make the following ten strategic moves to renew the credibility of the clergy amid a critical pagan public.

Refocus "the Call"

A major shift occurred between the first millennium and the second as the diocesan movement gained momentum. The "call" began to be defined by profession, office, task, and location. Today, most clergy and their denominational parents define their calling in the same way. They are "called" to "professional ministry." They are "called" to tasks of "word, sacrament, pastoral care, and service." They are "called" to a "holy office." They are "called" to a specific church that has a specific postal address and maintains a specific constitution and property. The very mind-set of "calling" lacks credibility to the public. The very self-understanding of the clergy lacks credibility, from the moment they are first interviewed by an ecclesiastical board and from the moment of their first conversation with the public.

In order to regain credibility, the mind-set of the call must return to its first-millennium roots. In the earliest church, people were called to a people or a microculture or a public. They experienced a "heart burst" for a definable, describable, identifiable group of people who desperately needed to experience Jesus Christ in a definable, describable, identifiable way. There was nothing professional about it. Indeed, one way to discern an authentic call from an inauthentic career move was that the true call almost certainly carried you beyond your level of competence. You had to retrain for it. You were not called to a task or a tactic. Your heart broke out of love for the Macedonians (Acts 16:9), and you risked everything you had to get to them. The tasks and tactics were unknown. The office did not exist. The postal address of the property did not matter. The apostolic leader simply disembarks from the ship (or unloads the family from the minivan) and figures out what to do in dialogue with the public and the Holy Spirit.

This shift of mind-set will have huge implications for the future deployment of clergy and the future practice of ministry.

❖ Candidates for ordination are no longer accepted into the process if they are merely exploring their spirituality or passionate about preaching and worship or excited about ministry. For whom does their heart burst? What Macedonian keeps them awake at night, or moves them to tears during the day? What experience of grace do they want to deliver that will give that particular Macedonian a good reason not to commit suicide tonight?

❖ Bishops can no longer move clergy around like pawns on a chessboard. At best, they can mentor the clergy to experience their heart burst, and they can recommend to the clergy a strategy to pursue it. The call, however, is not going to emerge from the cabinet meeting of the diocese, but from the hearts of spiritually alive clergy. The entire focus of the bishop changes. The issue is no longer which pulpits need to be filled, but rather which clergy are no longer spiritually alive? A spiritually dead clergyperson is an even greater liability to God's mission than a financially bankrupt church.

❖ The primary dialogue partner in the call process is no longer the church board. Instead, the clergy need to be in conversation with the public—the Macedonians in the zip code—beyond the church itself. At best, the congregational board can interpret the public for the inquiring clergy, broker wider discussions, and pray with the clergy about their heart burst and the best way to pursue it. The entire focus of the local church board changes. The question is not "Is this the right clergyperson for our membership needs?" The question becomes "Is this the right clergyperson to pursue our congregational mission?"

If a potential candidate for ministry cannot embrace the mind-set of mission, or if a local congregation cannot accept the primacy of the stranger, then they must be treated as Ananias and Sapphira. And neither the bishop nor the clergy should feel any guilt about it. Every compromise is a nail in the coffin of the church; every ruthless alignment with God's purpose to multiply mission is a resurrection for the church and new hope for the community.

Redevelop the M. Div. as a True "Co-Op" Methodology

Master of Divinity programs have tentatively experimented with practical theology. At the very least, they require a handful of hours doing "field work" in a local church. At best, they may require a year of full-time church work before graduation. The standard of learning expected from such field work is unpredictable, despite the best efforts of practical ministry staff. Placement is often a matter of expedience; churches are often just looking for inexpensive youth directors or pulpit supply; and evaluation is a distant second in importance to academic average. The demand for practical experience, and the discipline to combine practical experience with theoretical study, is nowhere close to the standard of any community college. This must change.

The M. Div. must be redesigned as a true "co-op" method of learning. It's not just that work and study should more equitably divide into 50/50 time management, but that work and study need to merge into a seamless experience of personal and missional growth. Less teaching needs to be done on campus than most traditional seminary professors assume, more disciplined reflection needs to be done on site than most field work placements assume, and it can now all be done in more creative, technologically sophisticated ways. Of course, this may extend seminary training—and the expense of seminary training—from three to four years. Yet local churches will be more interested in subsidizing bursaries for serious co-op education than they are now in doing so for ivory tower education that gives a condescending nod to the mission field.

Both the mind-set of academia and the mind-set of field placements must change if clergy education is to catch up with the community college. The church as a whole must surrender the Christendom assumption that clergy should be equal in status to doctors, lawyers, senior CEOs, and policy makers. The church must live up to a higher standard. Clergy should be truly equal in status to electricians, plumbers, human resource officers, medical technicians, and tradesmen. This means that higher expectations and greater accountability must be built into the field placements of the students for ministry.

This higher expectation and greater accountability in a true co-op education involves something more than a change in tactics. That is simple enough. The local community college system can teach us. What is more difficult to overcome is the hidden hierarchy of condescension and codependency that has been built up in Christendom between the seminary and the local church. Seminary professors can no longer be allowed to be condescending skeptics about the experience of Jesus, or the importance of Christian mission, regardless of the length of their tenure. They can no longer be as tentative as pagans in their church involvement and worship attendance, nor can they be inexperienced or unsuccessful in actual, practical Christian mission. They are either "in it," or they cannot "teach it." Similarly, field placements (local church, faith-based agency, or any mission unit) can no longer be allowed to be simply places in need of cheap labor or to be myopically obsessed by their own survival or tactical development. They must not only embrace a wider vision of Christian mission, but also must seriously accept the demand to participate in theoretical and self-critical reflection on-site. Either their mission shifts its focus from program development to leadership development, or they are dropped from the cooperative relationship with the seminary.

Require Apprenticeship

The logical extension of the seminary as a true co-op educational methodology is that the Christendom pattern of career development that has emerged in the second millennium after Christ must be broken. It is no use for the seminary to change its educational methodology if the established church does not change its leadership deployment strategy. At the moment, experienced and older clergy move up the seniority ladder from small churches to larger churches, and small incomes to larger incomes, leaving behind a vacuum that is filled by seminary graduates. They are often isolated and stressed, confronted by obstacles from which more experienced clergy preferred to flee rather than address, or picking up the pieces of abuse or failure that more experienced clergy have left behind. Alternatively, some newly graduated seminarians join the staff of a large church, but almost always to focus only on a specific program and rarely to experience further leadership development.

Some denominations have made ordination "probationary," pending further experience and assessment. Probation is an entirely different thing from apprenticing, however. What good is it to throw someone into the water without additional coaching on how to do the backstroke? Not only do many leaders drown, but the public becomes skeptical of the general ability of clergy to be lifeguards.

The obvious solution is that newly graduated or ordained clergy should spend at least three years *as an apprentice to a mentor*. This means that new clergy not only should serve in the mission field that is their heart burst, but also should never serve unless they work closely with a mentor who can coach attitude, integrity, skills, and teamwork. Training a larger cohort of veteran clergy who can work as mentors to new apprentices must become a priority for both congregation and denomination. As in ancient times, so also today: the credibility of the mentor is passed on to the credibility of the apprentice. What becomes important is not so much the seminary from which you graduated, as the mentor with whom you worked.

Probation may not be apprenticeship, but all apprenticeship is a kind of probation. This is not the time for isolation or individualism. It is a time for collegiality and experimentation. Every Onesimus, Apollos, or Lydia should be partnered with a Paul, a Priscilla, or an Aquila, in order to continue his or her maturation process as a Christian leader. The mentor/apprentice relationship is as unique as the individuals involved. Each searches for the other. The relationship cannot be forced, although it may be brokered by a denomination or seminary. The mentor's evaluation of an apprentice will be a heavy responsibility because the reputation of the one will be inextricably bound to the future reputation of the other.

Separate Vocation from Income

One of the second-millennium innovations of Christendom to New Testament mission was the notion that Christian vocation must necessarily be tied to ecclesiastical stipends. It was an obvious method of diocesan control. It withheld authority from volunteers, laity, and other "amateurs" to gather and lead faith communities. If you weren't being *paid*, you must not be *good*. The Christendom also checked overly zealous or maverick clergy who might breach the comfort zones of the established church. If you go too far, you won't get paid. This unhealthy connection between vocation and income must cease. Today the public concludes that if you are paid, you are probably not able or willing to be very creative. And they are right.

One way or another, the church must expand the authority of lay pastors, worker priests, and other missionaries to gather, shape, and lead creative new faith communities. The issue is not to give them a title or to slot them into a bureaucracy, but to give them authority and recognize innovative new missions. Many of the most credible Christian leaders today are not only nonordained, but also nonsalaried. They should be simply ordained and empowered to function with all the authority of a pastor or missionary. By all means, train them and hold them accountable to the mission attitude, high integrity, quality skills, and teamwork that one would expect of salaried clergy. Provide continuing education budgets, on-the-job coaching, and mentoring relationships. Let them earn an income on their own.

Would anyone do it? The diocesan church is skeptical, for who would work for the church if they did not get paid? The monastic movement replies that there are in fact *many* who are called and do *not* expect to be paid. Indeed, that is part of the credibility that they bring with them into mission. They are not "working for the church." They are following Jesus. This takes us to the root fear of the diocesan church toward the monastic movement: these followers of Jesus are willing to work for nothing other than for the love of the Lord.

One way or another, the church must surrender the assumption that every local church pastor, even in traditional diocesan church structures, *must be paid.* There are no "guaranteed incomes" today. Indeed, what we see happening is that there are clergy who are in ministry *for the income*, but *not for the vocation.* These are the clergy who prefer one appointment or job over another because it is closer to their home, is in a better school district for their children, is in a safer neighborhood, or offers a bigger salary. These clergy should be removed from the roster of available ministers. It is entirely possible that a church may call a clergyperson to lead it into ministry with a microculture and that together they may share a heart burst for mission, and yet the clergyperson will not be paid. The clergyperson's income will come from other work, in the manner of the earliest apostles.

The bottom line is that all clergy salaries demand a vocational heart, but not all authorized vocations require a salary. Perhaps instead of guaranteeing an income, the denomination or the congregation should instead broker a job placement service to help their genuinely, passionately called clergy get a real job while they lead the mission of Christ.

Deploy Pilgrim Bands and Plant Monastic Communities

The habit of the diocesan church of the second millennium has been to deploy individuals and plant churches. The habit continues to this day, even as the "church planting movement" explodes across North America. Much of that church planting is really no different from the second-millennium strategy. Take an individual, train him or her in new techniques, and help him or her establish a church that in ten years will look remarkably like other churches down the street only newer. Ten years down the road, the "church plant" will have a pastor with a guaranteed income, a variety of committees and line budgets, a multipurpose building on three acres of land, and a debt. *Voila!* A brand new Body of Christ *in residence!*

The new habit of the church should be to plant "monastic communities" rather than "churches." These are more innovative faith communities that may be embedded in any sector of public life (business, nonprofit, health care, and so on). Such communities would model high spiritual disciplines, share worship and the sacraments, live within Christian core values and beliefs, and aim to multiply disciples in the midst of their social service and business plan. Even if a newly planted "monastery" looks remarkably like an established church it should incorporate the same highly credible spiritual monastic leadership, discipline, and outreach.

The new habit of the church should be to deploy teams, or pilgrim bands, rather than individuals. Commission a team and send them forth. Instead of commissioning a solo pastor and expecting her or him to scramble about on-site pulling together a team, shape the team *first* and send all of them together into the mission field. Train them together, send them together, support them with a capital pool, and even encourage them to live in the same apartment building or house and eat at the same table. Pilgrim bands travel together for mutual accountability, mutual mentoring, mutual protection, and mutual mission. What they start out modeling, they end up establishing. The codependency between clergy and congregation is avoided from the beginning, and the high expectations for spiritual discipline are embedded in the foundation of the community.

Measure Disciple Making

Most of the statistics that denominations gather are useless to measure the progress of mission and to hold a clergyperson accountable for results. The diocesan church of the second millennium measured membership, operational budget, infant baptisms, generational group participation, regular financial giving, property maintenance, denominational support, clergy security, and congregational harmony. Unfortunately, every single one of these measurements could improve, and the congregation would still perish and the leaders still go on disability. The statistics that matter are regular worship attendance, missional budget, adult baptisms (unrelated to teen confirmation), affinity group multiplication, increased volunteerism, multiple sites of ministry, mission partnerships, the ability of clergy to learn from failure, and community hope. If these measurements are positive, then the congregation and the clergy thrive.

In other words, measure the integrity, intensity, and results of a *discipling process* rather than a membership assimilation process. Are people (and adults in particular) being transformed, grown up, mentored to hear their call, equipped to pursue it, and sent out in pilgrim bands? That is the information inquiring minds want to know, and not just the denomination. The public wants to know. Credibility depends on how effectively you give hope to the community, and not how effectively you maintain harmony in the church. If the church begins to measure the discipling process and hold clergy accountable for the number and depth of lives changed, people matured in Christ and participating in Christ's mission, and equipped missionaries sent out to bring good news to the world, then the church can make wise decisions about investing its limited finances, deploying paid and unpaid clergy, and initiating new strategies. The endless cycle of appointment-apportionment-appeasement is finally broken. It is replaced by an endless promise of call-empowerment-mission.

The diocesan church asks every question imaginable while interviewing clergy except the ones that really matter. Have you wrestled with and triumphed over the devil? Have you faced your inner demons and the spiritual enemies of Christ in culture? Have you revealed and accomplished miracles of grace? Have you taken people deep and mentored them to discern their own calling in God's mission? In other words, *have you multiplied disciples?* In the end, that is the only question that really matters.

The reason that the body in residence never asks this question is that disciple making might be offensive to the public, or at least to one public or another. Yet when it comes to the credibility of clergy, the public may well *disagree* with them, and they may well insist that they have the freedom to disagree with the clergy. But they still only *respect* a leader who knows what she or he believes and where the Christian movement is going. That's more than they see in the clergy today. They currently see the clergy making every attempt to build universal toleration, yet make no attempt to align themselves with a specific purpose. What exactly is the point of being a disciple of Jesus if not explicitly to encourage more people to become disciples of Jesus? Even if ultimately I would rather be a disciple of Muhammad, at least I know where Muhammad and I stand in relationship to each other. What the public cannot stand is a leader with no purpose insisting that everyone else should have no purpose, so that in the end we can all "get along" together. A leader with no purpose is an insult to the integrity of everyone else who has purpose. The desire to multiply disciples of Jesus may be a bad strategic plan to some, but it is a legitimate undertaking in the pagan world.

Break Control

The single most serious threat to the credibility of clergy is their inability to break control. The power to resolve conflict and increase harmony is neutral in the eyes of a skeptical public. Indeed, if conflict resolution deliberately clouds the single-minded purpose of the church to multiply disciples of Christ, in order to bring harmony through generally negotiated self-interest and shared purposelessness, conflict resolution actually undermines the credibility of clergy. The public all too easily sees the clergy as benign grandparents keeping peace amid a dysfunctional family, whose solution to every problem is more therapy, and whose primary goal is to seat everybody around a common dinner table on Christmas Eve. In the absence of a higher purpose, powerful or intimidating personalities are allowed to impose their personal agendas of taste, politics, and neediness on the rest of the dysfunctional family. So long as there is a veneer of peace, and the occasional new grandchild, the grandparent clergy are happy.

The clergy must be equipped and empowered to break control. By implication this means breaking the control of the family church metaphor; breaking the obsession with interpreting church life as family dynamics; and breaking the hold of intimidating controllers on the policy, program, personnel, and property of the church as if in the end it were all a family dinner table. The higher purpose of disciple making, and the accountability of clergy to that higher purpose, is only the beginning.

First, the denomination must support pastors as they break control. Do not allow controllers to manipulate you into removing or disciplining the clergy. Do not rush to impose a conflict resolution process. Instead, cooperate in identity discernment processes that build clarity and consensus about core values, beliefs, vision, and mission. Dare to remove board members, trustees, Sunday school teachers, worship leaders, and others from office if they fail to align with the mission. Support the clergy *and their families* with mentoring, networking, and emotional support.

Second, the clergy must confront control in the very areas where control is most excessive, obvious, and obstructive.

- **Worship:** The Sunday morning experience is the arena in which the true values, beliefs, vision, and mission of the church are revealed most transparently to the public. Credibility depends on the development of indigenous, mission-targeted worship options that are sensitive to the microcultures of the community beyond the church. The best way to praise God is to participate in God's love for the stranger. The best way to unite with Christ is to share in Christ's mission. Everything else is just tactics. Break the control of members who demand that worship shape itself around their personal tastes, political preferences, demand for attention, and family needs.

  The key to control is influence over music, symbol, and floor plan. All should be pressed into the service of a larger mission purpose to multiply disciples. Adapt the music, redesign the symbols, and make the floor plan interactive.

But understand that the real reason for doing this is to *reveal the hidden controllers of the church*. When they emerge, counsel them, educate them, or fire them.

• **Staffing:** The paid and unpaid staff must have authority to adjust the tactics of church life to accomplish the mission to multiply disciples. Credibility depends on the quality, relevance, and speed of the ministries of the church. While policy should be developed by the spiritual leaders of a church, program management should be entrusted to a gifted few. Most churches add paid and unpaid staff to maintain a membership assimilation process designed to satisfy controllers. Pastors need to add staff who will monitor a disciple-making process designed to reach strangers.

The key to control is influence over nominations and pastoral relations. These should be dismantled and converted into training teams and policy governance boards. The pastor should choose the senior staff; the staff leaders should choose their own teams; the team leaders should choose their own team members. Each should have authority to hire, train, monitor, and, if necessary, fire or dismiss the team members with whom they work. Management should never be done by committee.

Moreover, staff development should shape itself around discipling process, rather than around program perpetuation. Senior staff who work with the pastor (paid or unpaid) should include leaders for volunteer empowerment, operational administration, and Sunday morning experience design. Together they keep the discipling process that changes, grows, mentors, equips, and sends teams in constant motion.

- **Property:** The property must become adaptable, changeable, marketable, or upgradeable. Denominations need to encourage the renovation or relocation of church facilities, and congregations need to value adaptability over continuity. This does not mean the historic symbols are unimportant, but the power of any symbol lies in its ability to become a portal of meaning in the present.

The key to control, aside from the worship center, is the hospitality center and nursery. These are the areas that controllers most often use to limit access by the demographic diversity of the public, by making space too small, too inaccessible, too uniform, or too mediocre. Raise the standard of leadership for trustees and finance and property committees to increase their credibility as *spiritual leaders* through personal and small group disciplines. Require interaction with the public, demographic research, and worship attendance.

Control of worship, staffing, and property represent the most potent leverage points to shape the mission of the church. They are not surprisingly the most controversial and stressful aspects of church life to change.

Therefore, the credibility of leaders depends on the persistence, endurance, and focus of the church over an extended period of turmoil.

Reward Innovation

The church must learn the hard lessons that organizations in other public sectors have learned. In a world of mass migration, technological change, rapid communication, and spiritual searching, core values for maintenance, stability, and predictability are no longer practical. The church is one of the last holdouts in organizational America that rewards employees and volunteers for their *lack* of experimentation. Such behavior is quite contrary to the New Testament, in which Jesus uses the parable of the talents to urge an entrepreneurial spirit in the disciples. It is also contrary to the tradition of first-millennium Christianity, in which leaders of the Christian movement tried everything from funeral societies to house churches to table talk in the agora in order to share the gospel. It is the dominance of the diocesan church of the second millennium, and the need of diocesan leaders to control, that changed everything. Now we have to change back again.

It is easy to say "reward innovation," but difficult to do. It implies so many radical new ways of thinking. Churches must actually *reward failure*, or more precisely, they must reward the ability to learn from mistakes. Yet one cannot learn from mistakes if one does not have the freedom to make mistakes. And one cannot learn from mistakes unless the denomination helps clergy design strategies to learn from failure. This is a significant shift in thinking.

Rewarding innovation means accepting some strategic mediocrity. This seems counterintuitive to most diocesan church leaders, although it is obvious to monastic movement leaders. Some programs and ministries must be allowed temporarily to fail or diminish in quality, creating a vacuum for the Spirit to inspire new hearts, new ideas, and new visions that will adapt them to new contexts. Nothing loses credibility faster than mere perfection. Nothing gains credibility faster than a continuing quest for perfection.

Rewarding innovation means promoting the leaders who have a demonstrated history of innovation. These are the leaders who make mistakes—lots of mistakes—and who learn from those mistakes consistently. These are the leaders who are prepared to look like fools in the eyes of their colleagues and the public for the sake of a higher relevance in sharing the gospel. Ironically, these are not the leaders who grow megachurches. These are leaders who grow megamission. In order to do that, they risk downsizing their church in order to upgrade their spiritual rigor and mission focus.

Diffuse Authority

The great self-deception of the diocesan church of the second millennium is that the church thinks it has diffused authority by creating large bureaucracy. It imagines that it has truly empowered a diversity of leaders through representational democracy and parliamentary procedure. This is, of course, a charade. The only thing that is being diffused is the power to implement an agenda that a smaller power clique has devised. Bureaucracy retains the top-down control to discern, design, and evaluate mission. The charade is revealed in all of the meetings, reports, and liaisons. If authority is really diffused, then why do leaders have to attend so many meetings, write so many reports, and communicate with so many people outside their immediate mission? It is because they do not have the power they are purported to have. They must continually get permission, lobby for funding, compete for resources, and persuade someone else of guaranteed success. Even if they are successful in all that, their mission may still be terminated at the whim of an unseen hierarchy.

True diffusion of authority empowers leaders in every mission unit, great or small, to have real power to discern, design, implement, and evaluate mission without ever having to ask permission, attend a meeting, or write a report. Their accountability to the bishop, to the pastor, or to a staff person is only that they align with the overall mission, abide within organizational DNA, and refrain from doing certain things in the interest of safety, growth, and coordination. Authentic diffusion of authority is revealed in the lack of meetings, the absence of reports, and the reduction of liaisons. It is revealed in accessibility to capital pools, power to develop new resources, and freedom to think, speak, and create. Diffusion of authority does not happen through parliamentary procedure. It happens through trust.

Therein lies the profound credibility gap between the church and the world. The church distrusts the world so much, that in the end it distrusts its own people. The church knows that employees and volunteers, and even its ordained clergy, also are a part of the world. Suddenly they are all suspect. They must be watched. Any minute they will do something immoral, politically incorrect, dogmatically impure, utterly stupid, or really expensive. This fundamental lack of trust is the real cause for all the redundant levels of hierarchy, all the bureaucracy, and all the parliamentary procedure.

Reasonable trust requires more than clarity and consensus about the "DNA" of core values, beliefs, vision, and mission. It requires the creation of a corporate culture that regularly refines, aligns, embeds, teams, and targets that consensus. Denominational leaders coach pastors, pastors coach staff, staff coach team leaders, and team leaders coach teams:

- **Refine:** The coach helps the team go deeper in spiritual life and become ever clearer about DNA;

- **Align:** The coach helps leaders rigorously analyze every program and job description to deliver the shared vision and clear mission of the church;

- **Embed:** The coach helps leaders hold one another accountable to model the DNA in their lifestyles;

- **Team:** The coach shapes teamwork around the DNA, interfacing skills, getting results, and holding one another accountable in peer evaluation;

- **Target:** The coach helps leaders interpret the DNA for each microculture of the community.

The culture of trust allows the true diffusion of authority. Hierarchy can be flattened; bureaucracy can be eliminated. Leaders become free to function as autonomous mission units within a larger vision.

Divest

Historically, the chronic cause for the diminished credibility of the church among the public has always been its worldly wealth. Dante locates the greedy in the fourth circle of hell, and their peculiarly appropriate punishment is to be forced to push giant rocks in opposite directions. Their passion to "accumulate" things in life, which seemed so natural and easy, is countered by the labor of "setting things aside," which is now incredibly difficult. It is a morality metaphor for the church. Established churches of all brand names have amassed remarkable wealth, congregationally and denominationally, compared to the vast majority of people. They invent all kinds of excuses why they deserve to keep that wealth, and it is almost impossible to persuade them to let it go. But let it go, they must, if not now, then later.

It is easy enough to decry the amount of money spent in preserving heritage properties, redundant properties, or useless properties. The public understands that the church is really not in the heritage protection business and rightly discerns the hidden selfishness of the institution preserving empty cathedrals while people starve. Yet even the contemporary megachurch properties fuel the skepticism of the public. Such overhead seems excessive, comparable only to multinational corporations. The best one can say about megachurch property is that it is more marketable than a Gothic cathedral, but the public doubts that when push comes to shove they would sell it anyway.

Divesting itself of wealth involves more than property, if the church is to regain credibility among the public. It must also divest itself of its tax-exempt status and its privileged position in relation to the state. The flip side of tax exemption from the state is obligation to the state. Therefore, if the church divests itself of tax status, so also it must divest itself of civil responsibilities. Let go the obligations to perform civil wedding ceremonies. Let go the commitments to sign passports. Let go tax deductible housing allowances, book allowances, and study leaves. In a nation that claims to separate church and state, *separate church from the state!*

Finally, divesting itself of wealth implies a new purposefulness for all investments and endowments. Simply banking money or land against unknown risks that lie in the future lacks credibility in the eyes of the public. However, setting aside endowments for purposes of continuing education, leadership development, specific outreach ministries, and emergency relief is perfectly sensible to the public.

Property ownership by itself does not incur the skepticism of the public. Privileged property ownership does. Clergy salaries do not incur the skepticism of the public. Protected salary packages do. The public perceives the church not only as wealthy, but as intent on accumulating wealth. The protection of that wealth undermines the effectiveness of mission. Therefore, divest. Embrace the vows of relative poverty, or at least embrace a level playing field with all other public sectors. The public will respect you the more.

Building a Compulsion for Christ

At the risk of repeating myself: The path to clergy credibility is a straight line from the experience of Jesus to the mission of Christ. Any deviation from this path diminishes the credibility of the clergy. Yet that path is filled with temptations. How does one find Christ in the chaos? How do leaders build and communicate a compulsion for Christ and Christ alone? As church leaders look to the first millennium for guidance, and most particularly to the monastic movement, it is worthwhile to reread Dante. His *Divine Comedy*, written in the early fourteenth century, is perhaps the best story of credibility lost and credibility gained that was ever written.

Dante's allegory of progressive damnation (*inferno*), redemption (*purgatorio*), and salvation (*paradiso*) makes the central character (Dante himself) the very epitome of the cynical "seeker." He represents the cynical PCM (Persons of Christian Memory) and the alienated SYiA (Spiritually Yearning, Institutionally Alienated) publics. His setting is Italy in 1300; our setting is western culture in the early years of the twenty-first century. Both periods represent real and symbolic turning points in the history of the church. Dante writes with the Protestant Reformation looming on the horizon. We read him with a new reformation looming on our horizon.

Dante is thirty-five, lost in the woods, assailed by beasts, and unable to find the straight path. He knows there is a sun, but it is hidden behind a mountain. He desperately yearns for God, but he feels himself falling into despair. He is ruining his life, and he cannot help it. What an apt description of the twenty- and thirty-somethings today living in the wake of the boomer generation! They have dropped out of or have never known the church, and they regard clergy with varying degrees of disrespect or downright hostility.

Dante is rescued from his plight, not by a clergyperson, but by the revered classical author Virgil. Could it be that the starting place for the salvation of the seeker, the restoration of the clergy, and the reformation of the church lies not within itself but within the spirit-filled wisdom of culture? Could it be that clergy will be unable to reform themselves until they first look into the mirror of civilization, and that culture will be unable to redeem itself until it first regains its respect for religion?

My point is a smaller one, however. Dante applies the allegory to humanity as a whole. I only apply it to the church in general, and the clergy in particular. The crisis of credibility is more subtle, and the hope of the clergy is more complex, than we first imagine. We come to Christ, as it were, only after a long and dangerous descent into hell, a painful stay in purgatory, and a slow and disciplined ascent to God. It will not happen overnight. It cannot be accomplished by mere changes in church polity, personnel policy, or dogmatic theology. It is a journey both perilous and hopeful.

Inferno

The *inferno* describes the degrees of increasing disrespect the public has for the clergy. Virgil leads the skeptical and yearning Dante (the epitome of PCMs and SYiAs everywhere in every time) into the nine circles of hell. Each circle of disrespect is more serious than the next, until we arrive at utter hostility to the clergy and the church. Interestingly, the journey begins as Dante passes among people who had an opportunity to change and ignored it. This is unfortunately the majority of church members in our time. They have an opportunity to do good or evil and to unite with Jesus and participate in Christ's mission, and they prefer to ignore it. They are good people, but lukewarm people. Their punishment is eternally to follow a merely "white banner," symbolic of never passionately embracing any particular cause. They worship in sanctuaries that reveal a core value for beige. Dante, the skeptical seeker, shakes his head, exits through the back door without ever shaking hands with the pastor, and moves on.

CIRCLE 1: The Virtuous Unbaptized Spiritual Leader

The mildest disrespect of the public is directed toward spiritual leaders of any religion or virtuous CEOs of any nonprofit organization, who clearly do good deeds and model a good life. The reason they gain the disrespect of the public is that they are unable, or perhaps unwilling, to point the seeker *to God*. They are content to feed the hungry and shelter the homeless, but they cannot guide people further to eat spiritual bread or drink the waters that truly satisfy spiritual thirst for God. Innumerable nonprofit and social service leaders fall into this category. Their punishment, says Dante, is that they themselves can never see Christ.

CIRCLE 2: The Lustful Clergy

The second degree of disrespect is given toward clergy who are guilty of sexual misconduct. They have experienced intercourse with a consenting adult outside the boundaries of marriage. It may surprise many church leaders that the public actually views lust as only a mild sin. Current "zero tolerance" policies of the church are actually seen as an overreaction by the public. Love is a good thing, but it is sometimes misplaced. The public can accept that. Their punishment, says Dante, is that they are forever trapped in a violent storm just out of reach of their lover.

CIRCLE 3: The Self-centered Clergy

The third degree of disrespect begins to stir the real ire of the PCM and SYiA publics. These are the self-centered, or, as Dante might say, the "gluttonous," clergy. They are obsessed with filling themselves with good things and the perks of their office. They worry about vacation days, study leaves, Mondays, salary raises, health benefits, memberships at the golf club, honorific titles, and clergy vestments. They love to call attention to themselves and complain about how hard their lives are. The stressed-out public has little sympathy. Their punishment, says Dante, is continually to lie in the mud and endure cold and rain.

CIRCLE 4: The Greedy Clergy

The fourth degree of disrespect has already been named in the advice to the church to divest. It is greed, revealed in the accumulation of wealth, the protection of heritage property, and the need for tax-exempt status. These are the career-oriented clergy, always jealous of a colleague's appointment, and always climbing the corporate ladder. PCMs and SYiAs perceive them as no different from the average consumer. Their punishment is singularly apt. It is to push giant rocks in opposite directions.

CIRCLE 5: The Self-righteous Clergy

The public intensely dislikes judgmental and condescending clergy. This circle of hell is reserved for televangelists, preachers, and both right-wing and left-wing ideologically driven clergy. Dante says that they are forever "wrathful," harboring a constant anger against the world and everything in it. They are always critical, always solemn, and always demanding. They are particularly adept at manipulating people to feel guilty or experience shame. Their punishment, says Dante, is perpetually to fight one another in a fetid swamp.

It should be clear already that in the progressive disrespect of the publics that Dante describes, there is a movement from hesitant, benevolent regard to outright hostility. The lack of credibility for the clergy in the first five circles is rooted more in the passive, inadvertent, spontaneous, unreflective, or unintentional behavior of clergy. The further descent into hell reveals how the decline in clergy credibility is accelerated by what the public perceives to be active, intentional, willfully destructive behavior. Once again, the public imagination designs remarkably apt punishments for the clergy.

CIRCLE 6: The Heretical Clergy

Although the public probably has no real definition for the word "heresy," they can tell when clergy are clearly out of line with the bedrock convictions they are supposed to espouse. These are the clergy who take ordination vows and then violate them. They give assent to theological and moral principles about God's existence, Christ's salvation, or the significance of the sacraments, and then proceed to cast doubt, avoid mission, obscure faith, or denigrate spiritual custom. They *said* they were in essential agreement with the faith of the church, but clearly they are not. The public has no use for such hypocrisy. If you no longer believe it, then get out of the profession. The punishment, says Dante, is to be trapped in flaming tombs.

CIRCLE 7: The Abusive Clergy

Many of the most public controversies in both the fourteenth and twentieth centuries have been over the moral abuses of the clergy: sexual abuse of children, physical abuse of women, abuse of addictive substances, suicide, and anger against God. Dante divides this circle of hell into specific rings for violence against others, self, and God. Here, truly, the public expects a zero-tolerance policy. Yet, however public and strict the church may be toward lustful clergy in circle 2, they are revealed to be remarkably tentative and deceitful in circle 7. The "cover up" destroys the credibility of clergy. The punishment, says Dante, is (progressive) immersion in a river of boiling blood, entombment in a living tree from which their own corpses are suspended, and abandonment in a desert of raining fire.

Presumably, clergy in both Dante's time and ours are really starting to squirm, both out of a sense of their own culpability, and also out of a sense of increasing grief that agents of Christ's mission have let Jesus down so badly. The very depths of hell are reserved in the eyes of a critical public for sins of particular malice. It is as if clergy were the saboteurs of Satan himself.

CIRCLE 8: The Fraudulent Clergy

The other most public controversies in the fourteenth and twentieth centuries have been over the fiscal irresponsibility of the church in general, and of the clergy in particular. Dante's definition of "fraud," however, is more encompassing than that. He is thinking of panderers, flatterers, sorcerers, hypocrites, thieves, corrupt politicians, poor advisers, sowers of discord, and false witnesses. Anyone who deliberately subverts the effectiveness of Christ's mission is included. The punishments are many and severe, but the punishment of being bitten by snakes, and then being transformed into a snake to bite other villains, seems particularly appropriate to the public.

CIRCLE 9: The Traitorous Clergy

If fraudulent clergy sabotage Christ's mission, traitorous clergy deny Jesus himself. Judas resides here (along with Brutus and Cassius). Betrayal is hard to imagine. Once one knows Jesus, how could one betray him? How can anyone receive grace and then turn his or her back on the source of it? Once the public sees such calumny, they may never, ever come to Christ. That is why the punishment is so severe, namely, to be trapped in ice and be eternally consumed by the devil. The church in general, and the clergy in particular, may find that in the end hell is not hot. It is very cold.

Purgatorio

There is hope! Although Dante's *Inferno* is the section most often read and published, and although the imminent demise of the church and its clergy are most often confidently predicted, there is a route out. There is an escape. There can be a reformation. The credibility of the clergy can be restored!

In order to restore the credibility of the clergy and regain a compulsion for Christ, the church in general (and the clergy in particular) must experience the cleansing discipline of purgatory. Dante imagines these first steps toward redeemed credibility to be a journey of redemption as each of the seven deadly sins are overcome in turn. As you can see, the first steps toward credibility from the *inferno* parallel, in reverse, the loss of credibility as clergy descended into the *inferno*.

PRIDE: The Church Overcomes Its Arrogance and Condescension toward Others

This is the most deadly of sins, and the greatest liability to respect. The institution recognizes itself as an agent of God, not God in person. The clergy understand themselves as leaders among leaders, disciples among disciples, and servants among servants, allowing laity even to surpass them in ministry and mission. Clergy who were once bent over backward carrying the burden and responsibility for Christ's mission now stand straighter as they share the responsibility for mission with others.

ENVY: The Church Overcomes Its Jealousy of Other Churches, Religions, Public Sectors, and Leaders

Clergy no longer try to compete for income, prestige, influence, or power. They no longer vie with, undermine, or slander one another. They become open to conversation and ready to build consensus. They humbly understand that truth is larger than their opinions. Clergy who were once blind to the good in others now see with clarity and respect.

ANGER: The Church Overcomes Its Confrontational and Fractious Spirit

Clergy no longer resent their congregations and no longer lash out at the community. They lose their bitterness over being rejected. The repressed hostility that colors their behavior is healed, and they speak and act with unadulterated compassion. Clergy who once walked in acrid smoke now become a breath of fresh air.

SLOTH: The Church Overcomes Its Laziness and Spiritual Indiscipline

Clergy invest serious time in holistic health, disciplines of Bible study, intercessory prayer, faith conversation, and theological reflection. They start worshiping, instead of just leading others in worship services. They discipline life and lifestyle around the fruits of the Spirit and the experience of Christ. Clergy who once were continually running, everywhere, all the time, now shape their time management around their real calling.

AVARICE: The Church Overcomes Its Obsession with Property and Financial Security

Clergy separate ministry from salary. They no longer worry about fees for weddings, funerals, and civil services. They no longer participate in the consumer mentality of culture. They model financial and personal generosity. Clergy who once performed for a fee, now serve without charge.

GLUTTONY: The Church Overcomes Its Taste for Bureaucracy and Resources

Clergy no longer view others as a resource to further an institutional agenda, but dedicate themselves to helping others experience abundant life. They no longer consume volunteers, divert the spiritual gifts of others to achieve personal goals, or devour endless meetings. Clergy who once grew fat on the institutional diet now push away from the table and walk with Jesus into the world.

LUST: The Church Overcomes Its Desire for the Trappings of Religion

Clergy are no longer trapped in cycles of loneliness and longing. They rediscover healthy relationships and accept their own humanity. They learn to forgive and accept forgiveness. Clergy who once struggled with hidden passions find serenity in a deeper relationship with Christ.

One might say that there is an inward and outward discipline to the recovery of clergy credibility. The *purgatorio* is the inward discipline. It is what drives the monastic leader to the ascetic rigor of disciplining the body, mind, and spirit. All of the redemptive punishments of purgatory are aimed at taking back control of one's life and leadership. No longer driven by outward manipulations or by inner addictions, the Christian leader gradually restores the original unity with Christ that lies at the root of his or her original calling.

Paradiso

If *purgatorio* is the painful, redemptive experience of clergy coming to themselves and inwardly purifying their lives to be fit for the service of Christ, then the progressive stages of *paradiso* are the outward and visible signs of credibility that restore the respect of the public. Credibility has not been lost overnight. It has been lost in incremental stages through more than a millennium of institutional contentment and accommodation to culture. Credibility will not be regained overnight, either. It will be regained only through the purgatory of change in the inner life of church leadership, and then through progressive stages of incremental respect.

Is it possible to restore the credibility of the clergy in a single generation? Probably not. It was not lost by a single generation. Yet just as specific controversies and individual examples have accelerated the descent into *inferno*, so also specific victories and individual models can accelerate the ascent into *paradiso*. The one thing clergy must shed as they emerge from *purgatorio* is their modern sense of individualism. They did not cause the decline alone, and they will not cause the recovery alone. Each clergy-person is just part of a larger network of global Christian leadership and a larger chain of apostolic succession. You are more important than you fear; you are less important than you imagine.

SPHERE 1: The Renewal of Vows
(The Ideal of Martin Luther King Jr.)

You will recall the beginning of Dante's journey passed through the myriad of church members and leaders who followed the white banner of indifference. The first step toward credibility, therefore, is to replace the banner of neutrality with a holy quest. It is time to revisit and renew your vows of service. At the most superficial level, this means renewing the vows of ordination: the public confession, commitment, and consecration that is the foundation of church leadership. Such renewal of vows is rare today, but should become an annual occasion. It should become a ritual that is done surrounded by the monastic or diocesan community of faith, but also very much in view of the public. Do not renew your vows in the sanctuary; renew them in the food court at the mall.

This is the test and depth of your *resolve*. Resolve is no mere promise to do better. It is extreme dedication, and it is demonstrated by extreme measures. Monastic asceticism demonstrates the *resolve* of the penitent to surrender self to God's mercy and surrender lifestyle to God's mission. It is extreme. It may involve self-flagellation, hair shirts, fasting, poverty, and behavior that the world (and the diocesan church) may consider unwise or even insane. Yet this is precisely the extreme demonstration of resolve that will get the attention of skeptical PCMs and cynical SYiAs. In reference to my earlier diagram of two intersecting continuums of Christian experience, the "diocesan leaders in residence" of the established church will never break out into mission unless they *resolve* to do so.

There really is only one vow, whatever the particular denomination might incorporate into its ordination service. This is the vow to obey Jesus' words to "follow me!" No doubt there are times when it is difficult to discern where Jesus is going, or what faithfulness means in a particular circumstance. Yet these are exceptions to the rule. The truth is that instinct and intuition easily reveal the choices that must be made to follow Jesus. Along with resolve, you live by your instincts rather than by your rationalizations. Left unto itself, the human soul will always, always fly to God.

SPHERE 2: Doing Good for Its Own Sake
(The Ideal of Nelson Mandela)

The second step in the renewal of credibility is simply to start doing what is right consistently, persistently, relentlessly, and sacrificially. Actions can speak louder than words, and the public is watching you. Both in the daring intentionality of your deeds, and in the unthinking spontaneity of your behavior, do good. Reveal the fruits of the Spirit: love, joy, peace, patience, kindness, gentleness, godliness, and self-control. This may not distinguish you from the average Stoic or righteous pagan, but even in such company you are visibly distinct from the vast majority in the world.

Social service, justice advocacy, and prophetic activism can all accelerate the growing credibility of the clergy. Dante suggests that Christian leaders in this stage of the journey do good out of a desire for fame, but the nuance is ancient rather than modern. One does good out of a desire for a good reputation, a legacy that can be passed on in history, and public recognition of your association with the principles that give life. It is a positive notoriety that today is mistakenly interpreted as arrogance. Many credible spiritual leaders do seem arrogant because they stand up for a cause or defend a principle. They are uncompromising in their expectations and unswerving in their ambitions. The truth is that they don't really "like people" very much. They do love truth, goodness, and beauty. They do immerse themselves in scripture and lose themselves in action. Righteousness is an anomaly in the pagan world and calls forth respect.

SPHERE 3: Doing Good for the Sake of the Stranger
(The Ideal of Mother Teresa)

There is a higher motivation for doing good. It is the next step in regaining credibility. One does good *out of love* and not merely out of principle. Dante is a romantic and tends to associate such good deeds with action on behalf of the beloved. Yet the category of "the beloved" can be extended beyond those you know to those you do not know. Love of the stranger motivates good deeds. This is an eros, a passion, and a desperate urgency like that of a lover to work in the best interests of the beloved, yet applied to the stranger. It is radical hospitality, urgent outreach, and a heart burst for the "other."

This is more than righteousness. It is compassion. Doing good for the sake of doing good is the behavior of Amos. Doing good for the sake of love is the behavior of Hosea. If the clergy are to regain credibility among the public, then they need to learn how to *love* the public. They must cherish them in spite of their selfishness, wantonness, and ugliness. When the public mocks you, turn the other cheek. When the public persecutes you, forgive them. When the public rejects you, stay with them. Keep blessing the stranger, regardless of his or her receptivity or ungratefulness. Eventually, you earn his or her respect.

In reference to my earlier diagram of two intersecting continuums of Christian experience, the readiness to do good, either for itself or the other, moves the diocesan church to become a Body of Christ in motion. The faith-based, nonprofit agency and CEO begins to regain the respect of the public for the clergy.

SPHERE 4: Wise Teaching
(The Ideal of Billy Graham and C. S. Lewis)

Actions only speak louder than words for a time, and then you must articulate your faith motivation for doing them. Wisdom explains the rationale for the Christian life, points the way to Christ, and mentors seekers through the ambiguities of living. This is less about speculative theology than about practical faith. The clergy gain credibility among the public when they can teach others to do the good deeds and guide others to experience a heart burst for strangers. Wise teachers mentor more disciples.

The persuasiveness of wise teaching can only emerge on the foundation of spiritual resolve and good deeds. This is the point that often seems to be ignored among university and seminary faculties. Yet good deeds cannot maintain a lasting effect in society unless they are supported by wise teaching. This is the point that often seems to be ignored among social servants and political activists. Wise teaching merges historical perspective, human reason, biblical critical study, and the experience of the Holy Spirit to explain Christian faith to a seeking public.

It is no surprise that Dante populates this sphere of *paradiso* with the great scholastics and teachers of the first millennium and initial centuries of the second millennium of the Christian movement. We might well add more from Catholic, Protestant, and Orthodox streams of faith. Yet these are not just theologians. They are also evangelists and apologists for the faith. In reference to my earlier diagram of two intersecting continuums of Christian experience, the "monastic leaders in residence" draw people deeper in their understanding of the experience of Christ.

SPHERE 5: Courageous Action
(The Ideal of Dietrich Bonhoeffer, Rosa Parks, and Archbishop Romero)

The next step to regain the credibility of the public is literally to risk your life for what you believe. It is one thing to advocate and explain faith, and quite another to risk your life for it. The martyrs have always ranked high in *paradiso*, and Dante also locates the truly faithful crusaders among them. These are the saints who take spiritual warfare seriously, confronting the powers of evil.

Martyrdom has always been a powerful boost to the credibility of the Christian movement. On the one hand, no leader can confidently predict how he or she will react when faced with the possibility of death for the sake of Christ. On the other hand, leaders can prepare themselves for potential martyrdom in their careers, relationships, and legal status. The public respects corporate leaders who are prepared to be fired for the sake of a core value; civic leaders who are prepared to lose friends, spouses, or children for the sake of a bedrock belief; and ordinary citizens who are prepared to go to jail for remaining loyal to a larger vision.

In reference to my earlier diagram of two intersecting continuums of Christian experience, such courageous action is what impels the diocesan leader beyond activism to genuine crusade, and the monastic leader beyond the classroom to the gladiatorial arena.

SPHERE 6: Just Behavior
(The Ideal of Dorothy Day and the Anonymous Benefactor)

The restoration of credibility has so far been painstakingly achieved through attention to program and curriculum. The public can see the intentionality of your resolve, the strategic planning and deliberate action for good deeds, and even the momentary risk of life itself. Yet there is even more required of the clergy to regain credibility among the public, and that is doggedly to persist in the thankless lifestyle of just behavior. This is not about daring intentionality or careful planning. It is about constant, everyday standards of behavior. The credibility we have earned so far can be admired by the public, but the credibility that is demanded now must be imitated by the public.

Dante's sixth sphere of *paradiso* tends to be populated by ordinary people, but especially leaders who care about people of little means and few resources. Spiritual leaders treat little people with remarkable respect and sensitivity. They are not robbed, abused, mistreated, or ignored. This is religion on an hourly basis, a regular routine of kindness. The public respects leaders who shape their lifestyle around their mission. The Body of Christ *in motion* emerges as 24/7 Christianity.

SPHERE 7: Contemplative Insight
(The Ideal of George Fox and Thomas Merton)

Henry Wadsworth Longfellow captures the meaning of Dante's vulgar Italian in Canto 22 in his translation: "Then like a whirlwind all was upward rapt."[2] The public yearns for mystical insight and respects Christian leaders who can stand at the intersection of the finite and the infinite. Note that this credibility only becomes possible on the progressive foundation of the other six spheres of experience. The public will only cherish a vision if they first respect the visionary.

Contemplation is a paradoxical quality for a Body of Christ *in motion*. It sounds so passive. The mystical experience, however, recognizes that motion is a relative term. Up to this point, the credibility of the clergy seems to depend on their *personal* movement. They are constantly *doing things* and are respected as much for their energy as for anything else. The mystical experience reveals that the planets are moving as well. To say it another way, God's mission is what is in motion, and we are only a relatively small player in the process. We can be "still" and discover that the mission is still in motion. Credibility comes not through controlling the passage of time, but through recognizing the right time.

This is the heart of the mystical experience that is so highly valued by the public. If one can assign roles to the clergy, the first stages of credibility are "prophetic," and the later stages of credibility are "pastoral," but the emerging stages of credibility are "priestly." The body in motion is synchronized with the Spirit in motion. The clergy can point us in the direction of God.

SPHERE 8: Community with the Saints
(The Ideal of Albert Schweitzer, Desmond Tutu, and John Paul II)

Communion is the next step to credibility. The public yearns for authentic relationships that extend across space and time and that cross boundaries of politics and culture. This has always been one of the great attractions of the church in a world divided and torn. Yet it is not a community that is easily accessible. In Dante's allegory, he must first be tested in faith, hope, and love by the apostles Peter, James, and John. The public understands that if such a communion exists, it is no average community. They, too, must be "worthy" to join it and must hope that the clergy can open the door to such a communion.

The local congregation does not reveal the authenticity of the realm of God, but the realm of God can give authenticity to the local congregation. The clergy are a bridge. They prove that such a communion is possible. The depth and vitality of their relationship with the saints across space and time give depth and vitality to the relationships of those gathered around the altar. If the clergy are not in communion with the saints—if they cannot be tested by Peter, James, and John and proven worthy—then the congregation struggles to experience the depth and vitality of the real presence of Christ. If the clergy experience this communion with the saints, they transform the local church from flawed institution into a refuge open to all people.

True community is revealed in the experience of the earliest church after Pentecost, yet such community is blessed by the Spirit only if its leaders have been blessed by the Spirit first. The spiritual power of leadership unleashes the spiritual potential of community. Only after this long journey of credibility can the public really believe in the words of ordination for clergy. They sense the spiritual power of leadership and experience the door opening that will draw them into authentic community with the saints.

SPHERE 9: Participation in Divine Purpose
(The Ideal Adam and New Adam)

The loss of clergy credibility was a journey of increasingly violent self-interest and self-absorption. The regaining of clergy credibility is a journey of increasingly joyous obedience and self-surrender. Indeed, the very concern over credibility *in the world* is overcome by the joy of *alignment with God's purpose*. It is true that clergy should not worry about what the world thinks, but that freedom is not immediate. That freedom must be earned at the cost of discipleship. Clergy cannot glibly snap their fingers at culture and claim to be "not of this world," without having paid the price of service in sensitivity to the world. The public respects a spiritual leader who, in the final analysis, is serenely aligned with God's purpose for creation.

Dante's vision of the ninth sphere includes the praise of the angels and the recognition of God as the alpha and omega, the source and the destiny, of all life. Dante has forgotten all about *inferno* and *purgatorio*, until his spiritual guide invites him to look back in retrospect on his life (Canto 27):

> Whereat the Lady, who beheld me freed
>   From gazing upward, said to me: "Cast down
> Thy sight, and see how far thou art turned round."[3]

The credibility of spiritual leadership may be most purely revealed in how the clergy face death and the promise of eternal life. When the clergy step beyond obsessions with pensions, health care benefits, and retirement plans, and accept the call to "follow Jesus" as sufficient reward, and the public sees this in the most revelatory crisis of existence, they have come far, indeed.

CREDIBILITY AT LAST: Unity with Christ
(The Ideal beyond All Ideals)

The nadir of clergy credibility in the *inferno* comes as the public perceives clergy behaving in ways that are diametrically opposed to the nature of Christ. The apex of clergy credibility in the *paradiso* comes as the public perceives clergy to be united with Christ. The former is such a radical betrayal of all that Christian clergy supposedly represent it is hard to imagine they could ever reform. Clergy who are *unlike* Christ betray the implicit trust of the public so dramatically that it is seemingly impossible for the church to recover. Yet God's grace is working powerfully still, even among the clergy. Even the most disreputable clergy can be reformed. Clergy who are truly *like* Christ receive the respect of the seeking public. Their respect is not won because the clergy are always right about public policy, or because clergy are always successful in their profession, or because clergy are always busy doing ecclesiastical tasks. Their respect is won because *they are like Christ.*

Dante's journey of redemption ends when at last he sees Jesus. It is an experience with Jesus that he will never forget, that transforms his life, and that he will ever after be compelled to share with the public. He could not live without that experience of Christ; the public cannot miss out on that experience with Christ. In order to see Jesus, Dante changes spiritual guides for a second time. Virgil—the wisdom of culture itself—has guided him through the *inferno* and *purgatorio* of culture itself. Beatrice—the perfect woman, the bride of Christ—has guided him through *paradiso*. Yet it is the monastic leader, St. Bernard, who guides Dante in the final step to unity with Christ. Diocesan leadership gives way to monastic leadership. Only in such rigorous spiritual discipline can the clergy see the face of Christ.

In the end, the credibility of Christian clergy depends on regaining a compulsion for Christ. Credibility lost over the second millennium can only be regained through a spiritual journey in the third millennium, but for the individual clergyperson and the individual Christian church it can be a journey accomplished in a single lifetime. It will come in three ways:

❖ **Incremental Change:** Individually or collectively, clergy can reform themselves one step at a time, one day at a time, ascending the tiers of *purgatorio* and the spheres of *paradiso* once again to unite with Christ.

❖ **Apocalyptic Change:** Individually or collectively, clergy will experience painfully joyous transformational moments in which their hearts are strangely warmed, or in which their lives are dramatically redirected. These *kairos* moments are God's doing, bringing us closer to Christ.

❖ **Tipping Points:** Individually or collectively, clergy will suddenly be thrust into a new stage of spiritual and professional growth. Culture may do it. Spirit may do it. The clergy may do it to themselves. One way or another, they will be moved out of their comfort zones of ecclesiastical harmony and back into the crucible of the mission field where Christ is already waiting.

My particular focus has been on understanding the credibility crisis of the clergy, tracing the story of credibility lost and the possibility of credibility regained. Yet there is far more at stake here than the credibility of the clergy, or even the next reformation of the church. There is a connection between the lack of credibility for religious leadership and the lack of self-esteem in culture itself. The more religious leadership is in disrepute, the more culture itself becomes disreputable. Spiritual leadership and cultural self-respect are mirror images of each other. The recovery of credibility for religious leadership can signal the recovery among the nations of moral integrity and historical purpose. Christ really is in all, through all, and above all things.

Notes

1. See my books *Road Runner: The Body in Motion* (Nashville: Abingdon Press, 2002), *Fragile Hope* (Nashville: Abingdon Press, 2002), and *Mission Mover Beyond Education for Church Leadership* (Nashville: Abingdon Press, 2004).

2. See http://www.ccel.org/d/dante/paradiso/para22.htm.

3. See http://www.ccel.org/d/dante/paradiso/para27.htm.

● ● ● ● ● ●

Tom Bandy is President of Easum, Bandy and Associates (www.easumbandy.com), and an internationally recognized church consultant and leadership trainer. He has been a pastor in several contexts and denominations since being ordained in 1973 and served as the national officer for congregational mission and evangelism for the United Church of Canada in the 1990s. He is the author of over fifteen books and many articles related to church growth and congregational mission, and he works with congregations and judicatories across the theological and denominational spectrum in North America and Australia. You can reach him directly at tgbandy@aol.com.